THE DEMOCRATIC CHURCH

The
Democratic Church

DONALD E. NICODEMUS

THE BRUCE PUBLISHING COMPANY/*Milwaukee*

Nihil obstat: John E. Twomey, STL, Ph.D
           Censor librorum
Imprimatur: ✠ William E. Cousins
           Archbishop of Milwaukee
           October 22, 1968

The *Nihil obstat* and *Imprimatur* are a declaration that a book or pamphlet is considered to be free from doctrinal or moral error. It is not implied that those who have granted the *Nihil obstat* and *Imprimatur* agree with the contents, opinions, or statements expressed.

Library of Congress Catalog Card Number: 69-17320

TO MY WIFE, PATSY, AND TO MY CHILDREN,
MARY, DON, SHIRLEY, HELEN, PATRICIA,
MARTIN, AND JOHN

FOREWORD by Gregory Baum, O.S.A.

Catholics believe that the Church is God's creation. The Church's basic structure, including her ministry, is the work of Jesus Christ and his Spirit. Yet since this basic structure always exists in concrete historical situations, it is impossible to give an abstract, theoretical definition of it and to predict, independently from actual historical experience, the forms of ministry and government to be exercised in the Church of tomorrow. Catholics believe that the history of the Church is always open to the new.

The principle of development is generally accepted in the realm of doctrine. Theologians insist today that when the Church is faced with the new problems or enters a new culture, the doctrinal development is sometimes discontinuous. Positions affirmed at one time are qualified, corrected, and re-interpreted. The continuity of the Church lies in the self-identity of God's Word spoken in Jesus Christ and addressing the community in the present, to which the Church's doctrine gives witness in different historical situations.

While doctrinal development is universally acknowledged in the Church today, Catholic theologians are only beginning to reflect on the structural development in the Church. We have become so accustomed to the highly centralized papal government that we often forget that this government itself is the result of an evolution beginning from the diverse and loosely connected structures of the early Church. How did this development, including moments of discontinuity or shifts of orientation, preserve the self-identity of the foundations laid by the apostles? There is no abstract proof of this identity. What happened was that the Catholic people acknowledged the development as in harmony with the scriptures and their own Christian experience and endorsed it by an act of faith as the action of God in the community.

For this reason no theologian can answer the question whether the Church can be a democracy, in the abstract. While he believes that the Church's collegial structure (including the papacy) will always remain, he cannot predict, apart from the actual historical experience, how far the inherited structure can be adapted to meet the needs of a new age.

Thanks to Vatican II many democratic processes have been introduced in the ecclesiastical government. While there are now decision-making bodies on lower levels and public opinion is beginning to have some weight, the Catholic Church as a whole still appears like a monarchy. But for how long? There is no denying that the democratization of the Church, begun at Vatican II, continues. As this process goes on, at what point may the Church be called a democracy? Mr. Donald Nicodemus, the author of the present book, suggests that this occurs when the structure of society permits a consensus to form freely and to determine the policies of the government. We speak of a democratic society when there is an electoral process for choosing leaders and a juridical process for making decisions.

Mr. Nicodemus tries to show that we have reached a point in the Church's history where the convergence of several developments is transforming the ecclesiastical government and making the Church a democracy. In each chapter the author examines a theme that is assuming an ever greater importance in contemporary Catholic life and contributing to the structural transformation of the hierarchical Church. He deals with the recent thought on development in the Church, with the importance attached to personal conscience and the consensus of the community produced by the Spirit, with the deeper understanding of Church as the people of God in which all members have an active role, with the principle of subsidiarity which protects local communities from the centralizing tendency of the papacy, with the gifts of the Spirit and the need for non-conformity in the Church, and with the new understanding of divine revelation in its historical realities.

The convergence of the new thinking in the Catholic Church is overwhelming. There may be different schools of thought, tensions between biblical scholars and dogmatic theologians, theological differences produced by diverse philosophical methods; but on the issues examined by the author there is a broad agreement among the theologians publishing today. Because of the establishment of such a consensus the present study is a useful contribution to ecclesiology.

THE DEMOCRATIC CHURCH is an indirect refutation of Charles Davis' thesis that the Catholic Church is falling apart at this time. For Davis the Church is irremedially monarchical. Since for him the present system belongs to the essence of the Catholic Church, he regards the ills of the present system as sufficient reason for leaving the ecclesiastical community altogether. Nicodemus insists that the Church is not inevitably a monarchy. On the contrary, we are at this time involved in an historical process, sustained by several distinct influences, that is making the Church into a democratic society.

The new theological and ecclesiastical developments present in many parts of the Church have produced an extraordinary body of literature, scholarly and popular. Yet these developments have not been followed by the section of the Church that calls itself conservative. On the whole the conservative authors have ceased to publish. They occasionally complain about the new literature, but they no longer attempt to offer systematic presentations of their thought. They are not familiar with the critical biblical and historical method nor with the phenomenological approach that characterizes contemporary theology. Yet while these men are in a minority among theologians, they are still a majority among the hierarchy, especially in the Church's central administration.

The documents at present produced by the Holy See still reflect the highly conceptual theology characteristic of the past. At Vatican II the first drafts submitted to the Council were written in this spirit, but they were all rejected by the leading bishops on the Council floor. The official documents of Vatican II were on the whole written in the new spirit, aware of critical scholarship and sensitive to the historical reality of the Church. *The Constitution on the Church in the Modern World* was written almost totally in terms of the new phenomenological approach to theology.

Yet after the Council the Holy See has continued to publish documents written in the old style. What is happening is a certain estrangement between the Ecclesia and the Curia. We have begun to speak different languages. We operate with different sets of presuppositions. We tend to experience the Gospel in different ways. We communicate on different wavelengths.

Where is the present development leading us? If Mr. Nicodemus is correct, the convergence of several ecclesiastical trends will lead to a dramatic transformation of the Church into a democratic society. Why dramatic? If the Holy See continues to speak in a language removed from the Christian experience of the people, it may eventually produce documents that are no longer accepted by them. There is some evidence that the encyclical *Humanae Vitae* belongs to this category. This crisis of authority demands a rethinking of collegiality and papacy. It will be necessary to spell out the limits of papal authority and the share of the bishops and their people in teaching and policy-making. The present crisis of authority greatly promotes the ecclesiastical development described in this book.

By involving more people in the governmental process, by permitting the election of leaders and the formation of a consensus, the Church becomes more sensitive to the guidance of the Spirit who speaks to her through every one of her members.

CONTENTS

THE DEMOCRATIC CHURCH

CHAPTER I

PRELIMINARY CONSIDERATIONS

Monarchy and democracy stand in polar positions. Absolute monarchy, in which one person makes all the decisions, stands at one pole. Absolute democracy, in which all the people make all the decisions, stands at the opposite pole. In between are varying degrees of monarchy and democracy. It is not necessary that a government be at the polar position of absolute democracy in order to be classified as a democracy. There can be a *functional* democracy which, although not an *absolute* democracy, is nonetheless a true democracy (conversely, the same is true of monarchy). As a matter of fact, it would seem that in all but the smallest of societies a functional democracy would be superior to an absolute democracy. For it would certainly be a chaotic situation in which perhaps millions of people had to vote on every issue that confronted government.

A functional democracy delegates certain decisions to representatives, but invests the whole community with the right to alter or reverse these decisions. At some point along the line of democratization, a government moves out of functional monarchy into functional democracy. This point is reached when the structures of society allow a consensus to form freely and to determine the policies of government. This, of course, necessitates the election of representatives and includes the right of the people to reserve certain decisions to themselves.

Hence, a functional democracy is a system of government in which the common will freely develops and actually determines the decisions of government by means of elective and legislative processes. It is in this sense that the writer uses the word "democracy."

A government might be democratic in principle, and yet be something quite different in practice. For example, a country with a democratic constitution might have a populace in which 90% of the people are poor and illiterate. In such a case there might be no effective means of articulating the common will or of having it reflected in the decisions of government. Something similar to this condition now exists within the Roman Catholic Church. The basic principles of democracy are present in Catholic theology, as the writer will show, but they are not sufficiently applied. The *New Catholic Encyclopedia* states that in secular government, "democracy best fulfills the underlying principles in Catholic teaching."[1] Now, the writer's task is to show that even in *Church* government democracy is most compatible with the principles inherent in Catholic teaching. An examination of these principles will show that the theory of democratic government is implicitly present in Catholic teaching and that, if the present trend continues, a Church that is democratic in practice can be expected to emerge.

A brief definition of democracy was given above. A fuller description is now in order. The *New Catholic Encyclopedia* lists a number of characteristics that are "recognized today as essential elements in democracy":

> universal adult suffrage; representation in a legislative body of a fair proportion of the electorate; decision by majority vote of the electorate in determination of major questions of policy; equality before the law; equality of opportunity; freedom of speech, press, and assembly; freedom from arbitrary arrest and punishment; freedom in the exercise of religion; and the largest possible exercise of individual activity consonant with social requirements.[2]

---

[1] "Democracy," *New Catholic Encyclopedia* (New York: McGraw-Hill Book Company, 1967), V, 751.
[2] *Ibid.*

Though compatible with the principles inherent in Catholic teaching, some of these elements are completely missing from the life of the Roman Catholic Church, while others are present to only a small degree. "Universal adult suffrage" is quite clearly absent. "Representation in a legislative body of a fair proportion of the electorate" is far from being a reality, though the subordination of the college of cardinals to the college of bishops (demonstrated by the newly created international synod of bishops) is a sign of progress. "Decision by majority vote of the electorate" is absent from Church practices, but the more frequent sampling of opinion is a straw in the wind that indicates a drift toward decision by majority vote. "Equality before the law" will not become a reality until the executive, judicial, and legislative functions of government, now concentrated in the power of the bishop on the diocesan level and the power of the pope on the international level, are separated into relatively autonomous operations. "Equality of opportunity" within the Church is improving, as is evidenced by the increasing number of lay persons in teaching, administrative, and advisory positions; full equality of opportunity, however, demands that women be given greater freedom and that married people be admitted to the priesthood. "Freedom of speech, press, and assembly," though inadequately encouraged, is nevertheless developing; specific examples of this freedom are the *National Catholic Reporter* and the National Association of Laymen. "Freedom from arbitrary arrest and punishment" is guaranteed in theory by the Vatican II Declaration on Religious Liberty. "Freedom in the exercise of religion" is not yet adequate within the Church; for every priest like Father Groppi, who is supported when he exercises his freedom, there is at least one priest like Father DuBay, who is suppressed. "The largest exercise of individual activity consonant with social requirements" will not become a reality within the Church until there is a great increase in the number of relatively independent subsidiary organizations.

Although the Roman Catholic Church is not yet a democracy, it can hardly be denied that a certain amount of democratization has taken place. Democratization, obviously, refers to the movement away from monarchy toward democracy. It is a process of becoming. It is any change leading to a broader participation by the people in the decision making processes of government. Specific examples of democratization are as follows: the Second Vatican Council; the international synod of bishops; the National Council of Catholic Bishops; diocesan priests' senates; diocesan councils of religious; diocesan pastoral councils, which include clergy, religious, and laity; diocesan and parish school boards; parish finance councils; parish senates; lay controlled boards of regents at Catholic universities, e.g., Notre Dame and St. Louis; experimental parishes organized along democratic lines, e.g., the Community of John XXIII in the diocese of Tulsa, Oklahoma; the National Association of Laymen, an autonomous lay body consisting of 12,000 members in affiliated autonomous regional (usually diocesan) lay groups; the National Association of Priests; the National Federation of Priests (a union); the National Association for Pastoral Renewal, a group promoting optional celibacy for priests; lay controlled periodicals, e.g., the *Commonweal* and the *National Catholic Reporter*.

All of these developments, some more recent than others, have contributed directly or indirectly to a broader participation in the decision making processes of Church government. A development that has contributed directly to a broader participation in decision making processes is the National Council of Catholic Bishops, whose actions are binding on all bishops in the United States. Formerly, only the papacy had the power to bind individual bishops. A development that has made an indirect contribution to a broader participation in decision making processes in Church government is the National Association of Laymen. Their influence comes from lobbying with such groups as the National Council of Catholic Bishops and from statements and activities that mold public opinion.

Judging from the proposals that are being made, a democratization of radical proportions may be on the horizon. Such proposals come from a variety of sources, some prophetic and some institutional. A cross section of such sources might include William H. DuBay, founder of the American Federation of Priests; the Canon Law Society of the United States; the Dutch National Pastoral Council; and the National Association of Laymen. Specific proposals are as follows.

DuBay proposes the following: "freedom of speech," which would eliminate the prior censorship of books, "freedom of assembly," "full participation in the decisions of authority," "open financial records," "open personnel files," "adequate grievance machinery," "an independent judiciary," "full submission of the Church to secular law," thus eliminating tax exemptions on Church property and other privileges, "a constitution of the Roman Church."[3]

The Canon Law Society concluded, at its 1966 seminar on "The Role of Law in the Church," that canon law is in need of drastic change. Included among the recommendations issued were these: the separation of legislative and executive powers; an extension of juridical power by transferring the right to interpret Church laws from administrative commissions to high courts; the participation of the people in the election of their bishops; the full participation of women in Church life.[4] In October of 1967 the Canon Law Society sponsored a symposium which generated further proposals for the democratization of the Church. Most of the thirty-two scholars who participated in the symposium were canon lawyers. Two bishops were in attendance: Ernest J. Primeau, Bishop of Manchester, N. H., and Alexander Carter, Bishop of Sault Ste. Marie, Ontario, Canada. Bishop Primeau heads the canon law commission of the U. S. Conference of Catholic

---

[3] William H. DuBay, *The Human Church* (New York: Doubleday & Company, Inc., 1966), p. 171.
[4] James E. Biechler (ed.), *Law for Liberty* (Baltimore: Helicon Press, Inc., 1967), pp. 185–202.

Bishops. In a fifteen-page position paper the scholars urged the Church to abandon the monarchical Roman law system and replace it with a more democratic one modeled after the Anglo-Saxon system. The scholars called for the employment of certain accepted principles of constitutionalism, at least in an analogical way. They stressed the need for a separation of legislative, executive, and judicial powers. They asked for stronger guarantees of individual rights, including due process and equal protection of the laws. They praised parish, diocesan, and national councils as appropriate vehicles for broad participation in decision making processes. They viewed these councils as policy making bodies elected by and representing all parts of the community. Further, they maintained that their recommendations, if adopted, would serve to strengthen the authority of the pope and the bishops and thereby enable the Church to accomplish its mission more readily.[5]

In January of 1968 the Dutch Pastoral Council discussed a position paper recommending that the Church's leaders be selected by the entire membership of the Church and that the terms of office be limited rather than for life. The paper urged a return to the understanding of authority as service. Criticism was directed against the process by which Church authority came to pattern itself after secular authority, extending itself rather than working for the freedom of the people. The position paper was prepared by a national commission headed by Msgr. J. J. Loeff, secretary of the Dutch hierarchy.[6]

In September of 1967 the National Association of Laymen issued a set of position papers, one of which dealt with diocesan and parish administration. This paper called for: a legislative process in the Church that would be directive rather than advisory and that would allow general participation by Catholics in the formation of Church policy; the generalizing of elective processes within the Church, so that all members of the Church could participate in the selection

---

[5] *National Catholic Reporter*, October 18, 1967, p. 1.
[6] *Catholic Universe Bulletin*, November 24, 1967, p. 1.

of their leaders; a system of checks and balances between the various agencies of government; a greater degree of visibility for administrative processes, particularly in the area of finance; the establishment of autonomous organizations among the clergy, religious, and laity. The position paper maintained that the democratization of the Church would not weaken authority, merely change its form, so that it could be exercised more effectively.[7]

Although such proposals for the democratization of the Church are increasing, a number of obstacles might retard or even reverse the process of democratization. These obstacles will now be discussed briefly and later in detail. It should be understood, of course, that the writer discusses these obstacles within the context of Roman Catholic belief.

The first obstacle standing in the way of a democratic Church is the notion that the Catholic Church is perfect. The argument based on this notion runs something like this. Democracy is not possible within the Church because it is not compatible with the divine nature of the Church. If the Church is divine it is perfect. To change the form of government is to admit imperfection. Therefore, the Church cannot adopt a democratic form of government. This argument is based on an essentialist point of view, which considers the Church in the abstract or in its ideal form. The answer to this argument is found in an existential perspective, which views the Church as it is in the concrete. The Church is not only divine; it is also human. Because it is human it can (and does) have imperfections. Therefore, it is possible that the present form of government is imperfect and that another form is preferable.

The second obstacle is the argument that a democratic Church is not possible because the Church has never taught that democracy is a possible form of Church government. This argument is based on the concept that doctrine is unchangeable. The answer is found in the principle of doctrinal

---

[7] Position papers of the National Association of Laymen, September 30, 1967.

development. Certain beliefs are present in a germinal, or implicit, way and become explicit only after long periods of time have lapsed.

The third obstacle is the argument that a democratic Church is not possible because truth cannot be decided by majority vote. The laity, most of whom are theologically unsophisticated, would lead the Church astray doctrinally, as many decisions of Church government affect revealed truths. This argument is based on the false assumption that the pope and hierarchy alone are guided by the Holy Spirit. The answer to this argument is found in the belief that the Church is not simply the hierarchy, but the entire People of God, who share a fundamental equality. This belief implies that the Holy Spirit guides all the faithful and not merely the heirarchy.

The fourth obstacle is the notion that the hierarchy would not grant the freedom necessary to attain democracy. This notion is based on a faulty conception of religious freedom. The answer is found in the belief that religious freedom is grounded in the human person and is therefore an inalienable right. It cannot be conferred or granted; it is intrinsic to human nature and needs only to be exercised.

The fifth obstacle is the way some Catholics understand the obligation to assent to non-dogmatic teachings of the hierarchy. Limited in vision because of present preferences for monarchical structures, bishops may teach that monarchy is the form of government most compatible with the contemporary needs of the Church. Thus they would bind the laity to believe or to acquiesce in what is possibly an error. This reasoning is based on the mistaken idea that the teaching of the hierarchy always and necessarily demands assent. The answer to this argument is found in a true understanding of why a person believes. Assent is triggered by a convergence of probabilities, not the least of which are those arising from personal experience and reason. The hierarchy has no way of forcing a person to believe what his experiences and intellect reject.

The sixth obstacle is the way some Catholics understand the obligation to obey the commands of the hierarchy. Seeing democracy as a threat to their personal power and prestige, bishops might establish laws which would prevent a person from working toward a democratic Church. This argument is based on the faulty notion that obedience to the hierarchy is always necessary. The answer is found in the belief that conscience is the supreme guide in particular situations. A person must be faithful to his conscience even if it means disobeying the law, even if it means excommunication. Without police power, the hierarchy has no means of preventing excommunicated members from continuing their educational and organizational efforts toward a democratic Church.

The seventh obstacle is the argument that a democratic Church is not desirable because it would weaken or destroy the power of the Church to accomplish its purpose. This is based on the faulty notion that papal power must be absolute in order to be effective. The answer is found in the principle of subsidiarity. By taking care of the needs proper to their own spheres, subsidiary agencies (such as regional, national, and international legislative, executive, and judicial bodies) help the papacy function as it should and increase the power of the Church to achieve its mission.

The eighth obstacle is that the powerful bureaucracy of the Church can be used by bishops jealous of their power to stifle initiative that might lead to a democratic Church. Intimidated by the clergy, the docile laity would not have the fortitude to sustain the power drive that may be necessary to democratize the Church. The answer to this is found in the prophetic principle, which accounts for the formation of such men as Daniel Callahan, Michael Novak, and John Cogley (not to mention Jesus Christ, Martin Luther, and Martin Luther King). Ideas that are dramatically proclaimed can alter public opinion, rouse the masses, and produce institutional change.

Standing in opposition to each of the above obstacles is a

principle inherent in Catholic teaching. Stated succinctly, these principles are as follows: (1) existentialism (which in this book means only the antithesis of essentialism), (2) doctrinal development, (3) the equality of the People of God, (4) the personal right to religious freedom, (5) the experiential basis for assent, (6) the supremacy of conscience, (7) subsidiarity, and (8) prophecy.

These principles may be viewed in the context of recent shifts in the thinking of some Roman Catholic leaders and scholars: (1) from an obsession with the essence of the Church to a greater awareness of the Church as it exists in the concrete (the perfect Church vs. the pilgrim Church); (2) from a stress on unchangeable doctrinal verities to an understanding of doctrinal development; (3) from a notion that the hierarchy is the Church to a belief in the fundamental equality of the People of God; (4) from a condescending tolerance of those thought to be in error to a forthright proclamation of the inviolability of their personal right to religious freedom; (5) from an emphasis on the obligation of the Catholic to believe the Church's non-infallible teaching to a recognition of belief as a free act arising from experiential situations which produce a concurrence of converging probabilities; (6) from a stress on the obligation to obey Church laws to a recognition of the greater obligation to obey one's conscience; (7) from an emphasis on the supremacy of papal power to an acknowledgement of subsidiarity; (8) from a paternalistic demand for docility to a brotherly urging toward prophecy.

These shifts have brought certain principles into clearer focus, but they have not completely eclipsed those things which were previously emphasized. Just as that which has come into prominence was not altogether absent before, so also that which has been de-emphasized is not altogether absent now. For example, a greater acceptance of the notion of doctrinal development does not mean that there are no unchangeable truths—God is still the Creator, even though the seven-day creation story is recognized as a literary form.

What is happening is that new primacies are being established —freedom is gaining the ascendancy over, though it is not supplanting, the rights of the hierarchy.

The fact that new primacies are emerging is not clearly perceived by all members of the Church. However, even among those not fully aware of what is happening, widespread changes of attitude have taken place. The exact degree to which the changes of attitude have entered the consciousness of individual minds is not worth quibbling over. A new direction has been established. Those in the vanguard of renewal are fully conscious of these new primacies. As long as the present trend continues, it is only a matter of time until the new primacies are widely recognized. The more rapidly these principles become accepted, the more rapidly will the democratization of the Church occur.

The major task of the writer will be to show that the above mentioned principles are truly inherent in Catholic teaching. Beyond that, a supplemental task will be to indicate briefly how each principle provides, in effect, a rationale for the democratization of the Roman Catholic Church.

CHAPTER II

THE EXISTENTIALIST PERSPECTIVE

There are two basic ways in which the Church may be viewed —essentially and existentially. The former view points to the ideal Church, the latter to the real Church. The essentialist perspective sees the Church as abstract and immutable. The existentialist perspective sees the Church as concrete and changeable. The essentialist considers the Church perfect in government and therefore unable to adopt a democratic form. The existentialist regards the Church as capable of improvement, possibly by the adoption of a different form of government. Quite clearly, the existentialist perspective has gained the ascendancy in Catholic thought.

Bernard Lonergan, S.J., describes the essentialist perspective as classicist, conservative, and traditional; the existentialist perspective as historicist, liberal, and modern. He depicts the vast differences between the two perspectives. They differ, he maintains, in their understanding of man, in what they consider to be good, in how they understand the mission of the Church in the world, and in how they interpret scripture and theological formulations. It is a major accomplishment for one side to understand the other. The differences are basic and radical; it is a matter of total outlook. The traditional (essentialist) view, Lonergan continues, understands man and the Church in an abstract way through a definition. This view prescinds from the concrete, the changeable. It fastens on the general, the universal, the unchangeable. Man and the Church, viewed through abstract definitions, are understood as man as such and the Church as such. And because they are abstractions, they are of necessity unchangeable. The modern (existentialist) view, on the other hand, sees mankind and the Church as concrete collections of specific individuals. Mankind and the Church cannot be fully defined in abstract terms, because they continue to develop. The place of development is not to be found in the context of fixed ideas, but in the shifting context of meaningful encounters that arise from environment. The traditional (essentialist) mode of thought focuses on abstractions and does not lead to an awareness of the necessity for legal, structural, and methodological change. Universals remain the same. The Church as such never changes. Man as such never changes. For change can occur only in the concrete. The modern (existentialist) perspective focuses on the world of common experience, not exclusively on the definition derived from a limited cultural and theological heritage. The common meanings that are produced by common experience are not a supply of ideal forms existing in Plato's heaven. They are the product of man's evolving understanding of nature. As Lonergan sees it, the traditional (essentialist) view does not find its origin in sound theology, but rather in a certain philosophic or scientific conception of reality that is now suspect. Certainly, it has no basis in scripture, and scripture scholars repudiate it for its abstractness and for its omissions.[1]

The existentialist perspective has clearly gained the ascendancy among bishops and theologians in the Roman Catholic Church. This is evidenced by the voting at the Second Vatican Council and by the writings of such individuals as Bernard Lonergan, S.J., Edward Schillebeeckx, O.P., Daniel O'Hanlon, S.J., Henri Bouillard, S.J., Michael Novak, Daniel Callahan, Gregory Baum, O.S.A., Stephen Laszlo, and Karl Rahner, S.J.

Edward Schillebeeckx, O.P., sees the two perspectives as the

---

[1] Bernard Lonergan, S.J., "The Transition from a Classicist World-View to Historical Mindedness," *Law for Liberty*, ed. James E. Biechler (Baltimore: Helicon Press, Inc., 1967), pp. 126–133.

basic cause of the division of the Council Fathers of Vatican II into two camps. The essentialists prepared the early schemata in traditional jargon peculiar to their mentality. The first large-scale vote indicated that the pronouncements of Vatican II would be written from an existentialist perspective. In effect, 63 per cent of the world episcopate voted to reject the essentialist point of view. While it is encouraging that such a high percentage of bishops possess an existentialist perspective, it is nonetheless disturbing that such a sizable minority is enslaved by the rigidity of the essentialist viewpoint. "For at least 63 per cent of the world episcopate," says Schillebeeckx, "the Church's salvation lies along paths quite different from those of the remaining 37 per cent." Particularly confusing to Schillebeeckx is the ease with which the essentialist bishops reject the thinking of the majority. Although the vote made clear that the majority of the bishops of the world had forsaken the essentialist perspective, the essentialist bishops did "not even for a moment begin to doubt their own ideas." Perhaps the essentialists subconsciously regard the existentialists as heretics. This explanation by Schillebeeckx is offered in a somewhat uncertain way as perhaps the ultimate and logical conclusion of essentialist thinking. Apart from this explanation, it seems that the intransigence of the essentialist bishops toward the majority thinking is incomprehensible.[2]

In contradistinction to the closedmindedness of the essentialists, the existentialists are characterized by an openness that concerns itself primarily with the afterlife. Ecumenist Daniel J. O'Hanlon, S.J., sees this stress on the here-and-now as opening new areas of agreement with other believers. In *Current Trends in Theology* O'Hanlon writes that *Mater et Magistra* and *Pacem in Terris* are expressions of Pope John's concern for the here-and-now, for the "realities of this world."[3]

Defenders of the essentialist position reject the existentialist viewpoint because they think it is completely foreign to the

---

[2] Edward H. Schillebeeckx, O.P., *The Layman in the Church* (Staten Island, New York: Alba House, 1963), pp. 9–13.

[3] Donald J. Wolf, S.J., and James V. Schall, S.J., (eds.), *Current Trends in Theology* (New York: Doubleday & Company, Inc., 1966), p. 29.

tradition of the Church and therefore a corruption of doctrine. Those in the existentialist camp argue that although their perspective has often been submerged in the past, it is an integral part of the best tradition of the Church. Karl Rahner, S.J., for example, sees the existentialist position dominating the writings of Thomas Aquinas. Discussing Rahner's doctoral dissertation on Thomas Aquinas, Herbert Vorgrimler, S.J., says that for Aquinas "the metaphysical or finite knowledge is the first approach to philosophical reflection." Rahner proves, says Vorgrimler, that in the Thomistic synthesis "man's knowing takes place first and foremost in the world of experience, since the human mind is constantly turned toward the outward appearance." Vorgrimler quotes the concluding remarks of Rahner's dissertation: "Aquinas's epistemology is Christian in as much as it recalls man to the here and now of his finite world."[4]

The existentialist perspective is seen by its proponents as necessary for a proper understanding of even the basic concepts of theology. Henry Bouillard, S.J., says in "Human Experience as the Starting Point of Fundamental Theology" that if Catholics are to explain the meaning of human existence to others, the Christian message must be presented in terms that open themselves to all men, not just to those familiar with conceptualist jargon. The Christian message, he says, must be confronted "with the internal logic of human experience." The result of this confrontation should not be a system of abstract "truths immanent in human nature." Such a system precludes the gratuitous and transcendent action of a God who cannot be limited by the finitude of mental constructs. It is the task of fundamental theologians, while remaining faithful to what has been revealed, to show that human experience is open to a free intervention by a transcendent God in human history. The base, therefore, from which fundamental theology must proceed is the bedrock of man's experience. Such an approach reveals both the negative and positive aspects of

---

[4] Herbert Vorgrimler, *Karl Rahner: His Life, Thought and Works,* trans. Edward Quinn (Glen Rock, N.J.: Paulist Press, 1966), pp. 21–23.

the human situation—man's kindness and man's cruelty,
man's virtues and man's vices.[5]

Further evidence that the existentialist perspective has taken
hold in the Roman Catholic Church may be found in the
criticism of abstract formulas. According to Michael Novak
in *The Open Church,* the abstract jargon used by Catholics
opens them to the charge of "double-think." He cites three
examples of abstract jargon that particularly irritate him,
namely, "that the Church is sinless, essentially never changes,
possesses the whole truth." His trenchant remarks about the
sinful Church conclude with the statement that the Church is
not mythical, but incarnate, concrete, real, and individual.
He then points out that the essentials of the Church *have*
changed. It required many centuries for collegiality to sink
into oblivion, for the primacy of Rome to develop, for the
diaconate to shrink to insignificance, for the canon of scripture to be finalized, for the sacraments to be formalized and
distinguished from one another and from other signs. In examining the notion that the Church has the "whole truth," Novak
mentions the obvious fact that the whole truth was not evident
at the Second Vatican Council. Even on major issues, the
bishops disagreed with one another. In the concrete, no one
in the Church possesses the whole truth. The world of the
imagination may harbor "a perfect Church, full of truth,
never changing," but this is not the Church that exists in "the
concrete world of history."[6]

Obviously indebted to Lonergan, Novak places a premium
on the drive to understand and on insight. He maintains that
the closed Church of pre-Vatican II days was characterized by
an obsession with abstractions and by a neglect of insight.
Words, formulas, and conceptions were used to construct walls
of separation, one wall cutting off the insights of the outside
world of thought, another wall cutting off the insights of the

[5] Johannes B. Metz (ed.), *The Church and the World,* Vol. VI of
Concilium, ed. Edward Schillebeeckx, O.P., *et al.* (New York: Paulist
Press, 1965), pp. 90–91.
[6] Michael Novak, *The Open Church* (New York: The Macmillan Company, 1962), pp. 349–352.

conceptualist world. A world of thought that is merely conceptual is confining. However, living insight, which follows
upon the drive to understand the concrete world of experience,
gives one the freedom of two worlds—that of the concept and
that of insight.[7]

The drive to understand, says Novak, leads religious men
to re-examine and correct their own reflections. Otherwise,
a limited conception of God (which all human knowledge of
him is) might grow into an idol. Maturity for the individual
and the community depends upon fidelity to the drive to
understand and also upon the elimination of "counter-rational
patterns" of thought, which set up formulas or abstractions as
idols.[8] Novak believes that conceptualist thinking has begun to
give way to the drive to understand and to living insight. He
says that Pope John founded the Second Vatican Council on
the "principle of historical development and the principle of
concrete reality."[9] And Pope Paul VI implicitly recognized
the drive to understand when, at both the opening and closing
addresses of the second session, he said that the Church is
attempting to gain a new consciousness of herself.[10]

Much of the official language of the Church reflects a
strong essentialist perspective, though the statements of
Vatican II are an exception. In *Honesty in the Church* Daniel
Callahan criticizes the Church's official language, contending
that in its present form it is not a satisfactory vehicle for
conveying the whole truth. It does not lend itself to public
recognition of guilt. It presents an exalted image of the
Church that is inconsistent with her pilgrim nature. A prelate
he quotes describes the Church as "replendent and regal" in
countenance, and "in regard to things temporal . . . the source
of benefits as manifold and great as if the chief end of her
existence were to insure the prospering of our earthly life."
In one sense, says Callahan, this description is true, but it is
also misleading. It has faulty implications (e.g., triumphalism)

---

[7] *Ibid.*, p. 347
[8] *Ibid.*, p. 345.
[9] *Ibid.*, p. 55.
[10] *Ibid.*, p. 346.

and serious omissions (e.g., a penitent spirit). It implies that the chief objective of the Church is to promote our material welfare. It omits any trace of admission that the Church is sinful. Since the Church is both holy and sinful, the official language of the Church ought to proclaim both realities. The whole truth needs to be asserted. Anything less is dishonest and unrealistic.[11]

The essentialist viewpoint sees the Church primarily as institution and minimizes its non-institutional aspects. Fortunately, this perspective is being replaced by an existentialist outlook. Evdence that a shift is occurring is found in the writings of progressive theologians like Gregory Baum, O.S.A. He is critical of those who overemphasize the institutional aspects of the Church. He does not deny the importance of the institution. And he grants the institutional perfection of the Roman Catholic Church. That is, he believes the Church has an apostolic hierarchy, an integral doctrine, and seven sacraments (although the language seems to imply it, an institutionally perfect Church is not one in which the hierarchy has no sinners, or in which the doctrine is fully understood, or in which the sacraments are received with the proper disposition). By definition these three things (hierarchy, doctrine, sacraments) constitute the institution of the Church. However, Baum is quick to point out that the institution is not the only aspect of the Church, or even the most important. He contends that the skeletal institution is less important than the dynamic body. The crucial thing for Baum is whether the Church is concretely, or actually, functioning as it should. He maintains that although a Church not in union with Rome is *institutionally* an imperfect realization of the Church of Christ, such a Church may *actually* realize the Church of Christ in a fuller manner than a Church which is in union with Rome.[12]

---

[11] Daniel Callahan, *Honesty in the Church* (New York: Charles Scribner's Sons, 1965), p. 135.
[12] Gregory Baum, O.S.A., "The Ecclesial Reality of the Churches," *The Church and Ecumenism,* ed. Hans Küng, Vol. IV of *Concilium,* ed. Edward Schillebeeckx, O.P. *et al.* (New York: Paulist Press, 1965), p. 82.

More important than what a person has is what he does with his possessions. The same is true for the Church. While it is true that the institution has facilitated the development of the Roman Church, the thing of crucial significançe is whether a person or a church responds here and now to the promptings of the Spirit. At this point one is reminded of Jesus' reply to the person who said, "Blessed is the womb that bore you and the breasts that nursed you." And Jesus replied, "Say, rather, blessed are those who hear the word of God and keep it." Biological life is secondary to spiritual life, even in the mother of Jesus. The institution is secondary to the free outpourings of the Spirit, even in the Roman Church.

Perhaps the clearest indication that the essentialist perspective has lost ground is found in the widespread recognition that the Church is sinful. Although Catholics have long recognized that man is weak and sinful, they have for centuries been reluctant to describe the Church in such terms. They have tended to view the Church in an ideal and unrealistic way that reveals the virtues and obscures the vices. To suggest even now to Catholics that the Church is sinful is to arouse feelings of uneasiness and insecurity. Prior to Vatican II such a suggestion frequently aroused not only uneasiness, but positive resentment, hostility, and even contempt. A realistic word has transformed more than one devout gaze into a seething stare of hatred. It has taken Catholics a long time to return to an earlier awareness of the sinfulness of the Church. Finally, however, they are facing up to this sad and ugly fact. The Constitution on the Church is an example of this greater awareness. It describes both the strengths *and* the weaknesses of the People of God: "The Church . . . is at the same time holy and always in need of being purified, and incessantly pursues the path of penance and renewal" (♯8).[13]

While the above document clearly stresses the sinfulness of the Church, it does so rather succinctly. The speeches on

---

13 Walter M. Abbott, S.J. (ed.), *The Documents of Vatican II* (New York: Guild Press, 1966), p. 24.

the council floor were sometimes much more elaborate on this point and often more candid. An example would be the speech given by Bishop Stephen Laszlo of Eisenstadt, Austria, entitled "Sin in the Holy Church of God." He insisted on the regularity with which the People of God stray from the Lord. The Church desires to be faithful, but is found guilty of infidelity again and again. It wants to be holy and just, but repeatedly is sinful and the recipient of God's anger. People with broad experience in the world are aware that there is a contradiction between the way Churchmen describe the Church and the way the Church actually performs. Although "theology seems to describe a Church of saints," says Laszlo, "life itself seems to show us a Church of *sinners*." Because the Church is sinful, it is always in need of God's mercy and help. While both Christ and the People of God intend the Church to be in the communion of saints, it is more accurately described as a communion of penitents. "In actual fact," says Laszlo, "in this present state on the way to God it always turns out by the malice of men to be also a communion of sinners."[14]

Careful to distinguish between the Church and its members, Catholics have argued that the Church is holy and only the members are sinful. Since the Church is Christ and Christ cannot be sinful, the argument goes, the sin must be found in the people, not the Church. But this is an essentialist argument, which has lost support among the majority of the bishops. Karl Rahner, S.J., is quite plain about the matter: "The Church is sinful." It is not simply that sinners are in the Church in a way that imputes nothing to the Church. Rather, what can be said about the members can be said about the Church. One may have an ideal conception of the Church, Rahner acknowledges, but he maintains that this is not the real Church. The real Church is the visible Church, the sum total of the baptized. For Rahner it is simply a matter of

---

[14] Hans Küng, Yves Congar, O.P., and Daniel O'Hanlon, S.J. (eds.), *Council Speeches of Vatican II* (Glen Rock, New Jersey: Paulist Press, 1964), pp. 44–46.

cold logic—if the members are sinful, then the Church is sinful:

> If she is something real, and if her members are sinners and as sinners remain members, then she is herself necessarily sinful. Thus the sin of her children is spot and stain even on the Mystical Body of Christ. The Church is a sinful Church: it is part of her creed and no mere conclusion of experience. And it is terrifying.[15]

Rahner goes on to say that if the Church is conceived as mother, one must not deny her faults: "The sincere believer will see sins and stains, scandal and rebellion in his mother." The mature Christian does not attempt to hide or minimize the sin of mother Church. If the Church is to be made manifest to the world, her face and therefore her sin cannot be hidden. In truth, the countenance of our Holy Mother bears the unmistakable effects of sin. Her countenance reflects the sin that infects the members of her body and gives her the appearance of a leper. She has many sins—"the sad realities of pride, vanity, commercialism, imperiousness, gossiping, double-bookkeeping, narrowness," not to mention the more hideous ones.[16]

Attempts to conceal the sins of the Church are to no avail, for truth will out. As Rahner puts it, there are always Scribes and Pharisees ready to drag the "sinful woman" before the Lord and accuse her of adultery. But as the adulteress stands before the Lord in open but humble profession of guilt, her deeper holiness comes to light. And just as it would be unrealistic to deny her sin, it would also be unrealistic to deny her simple virtue. Rahner becomes poetic at this point. He depicts the Church as it will be at the end of time, when the final accounting is to be made. Standing repentant before the Lord, the Church is aware of her sins and reflects only upon her guilt. The Lord knows her sins more than any of those who want to stand in judgment of her. In silence he writes her sins in the sands of history, which along with her guilt will be rubbed out. One by one her ac-

---

15 Karl Rahner, S.J., "The Church of Sinners," *Cross Currents*, I (Spring, 1951), 68–69.
16 *Ibid.*, pp. 72–73.

cusers pass by, and finally she is alone with Jesus. Looking
into her eyes, the Lord asks whether any man has condemned
her. Remorsefully, she replies: No one, Lord. And he says:
Then neither will I. Finally, kissing her brow, he greets her as
his spouse and his holy Church.[17]

It is quite clear from what has been said above that a shift
has occurred in the thinking of the Roman Catholic Church—
the essentialist perspective has declined and the existentialist
perspective has grown. The shift is not complete, however.
As Schillebeeckx said in a passage quoted above, a sizeable
minority of the Council Fathers retained the essentialist point
of view. Churchmen of this mind can obstruct change, but
since they are no longer the dominant force the obstacles they
present are not irremovable. The principle of existentialism
(or realism or whatever it might be called) has been firmly
established. This means that a Catholic need not be chained to
abstract or ideal notions that exclude the possibility of a democratic Church. Whereas the essentialist conception of the
Church would seem to exclude a democratic form of government, the existentialist viewpoint allows such an adaptation.

Because the existentialist perspective brings into focus the
sinfulness of the Church, the movement toward a democratic
Church can be expected to grow. For as more and more
Catholics recognize the sins and weaknesses of the Church,
there will be more discussion about the kind of government
most able to promote the work of the Church among its sinful
people. This may lead many Catholics to work for democracy
in the Church, as democracy seems to be the best form of
government yet devised to guard against the great wickedness
of which man is capable.

Reinhold Niebuhr says: "Man's capacity for justice makes
democracy possible; but man's inclination to injustice makes
democracy necessary."[18] Individually, man is capable of great
wickedness, but, collectively, he is capable of indescribable
horror. As Niebuhr points out, man is interested in more than

---

[17] *Ibid.,* p. 74.
[18] Reinhold Niebuhr, *The Children of Light and the Children of Darkness*
(New York: Charles Scribner's Sons, 1960), p. xi.

mere physical survival. He craves prestige and social acceptance. Anticipating the perils which may befall him, he guards
against them by building power and security, both individually
and collectively. He is haunted by a sense of insignificance and
tends to negate this feeling by developing an inordinate pride.
The conflicts between men, Niebuhr contends, are never
simple struggles for survival in which opposing forces see each
other objectively. Each side seeks to protect its power and
prestige. Each side exaggerates its own virtues and the other's
vices. It is a very complicated struggle with ulterior motives.
And when the struggle is collective, cruelty escalates. No evil
is too great to be inflicted by a fascist state upon its enemies.
And now that technology has developed, there is a potentiality
for inhumanity that infinitely surpasses anything that history
has thus far produced.[19]

The collective form of evil expresses itself in all human
structures, including those of the Church. To repeat the words
of Rahner, the Church is sinful and it is frightening. When
individual and collective evils build themselves into the
Church, a kind of paralysis sets in. Sins of omission abound.
There is, in such a situation, little the Church can do or say
about the evils that mount in the broader community of man.
It may not be evident that evils in society are often present
because of cowardice and silence in the Church, for the
Church may amidst great degradation appear as a tower of
righteousness. Neglecting weightier matters, the Church can
give itself to public displays of petty generosity and righteous
indignation about trivialities. But whether the sin of the
Church is one of omission which is unrecognized or whether
it is one of commission which is evident to all (as was the
Inquisition), the evil is present in the Church. To guard
against this evil, which penetrates every level of the Church,
including the pope and bishops, a democratic form of government seems necessary. Perhaps a superior kind of government
will arise in the future, but for the present, democracy appears to be best able to promote the common good among
sinful men, both in the world and in the Church.

---

[19] *Ibid.*, pp. 20–23.

CHAPTER III

THE PRINCIPLE OF
DOCTRINAL DEVELOPMENT

The Church cannot become a democracy, some would argue, because the Church has never taught that democracy is a desirable form of Church government. The principle of doctrinal development provides an answer to this argument. If the doctrine of the Church did not admit of development, such an argument might be valid. But the principle of doctrinal development is now well established in Catholic thought. Because of this principle it is at least theoretically possible that Catholic doctrine could develop to the point where democracy would be widely accepted as the form of Church government most compatible with the nature of the Church.

This chapter intends to show that the principle of doctrinal development is firmly established within the Roman Catholic Church and that the acceptance of this principle is due in large measure to the pressure of external forces. This will provide the basis for the conclusion that a democratic form of Church government is both possible and desirable.

Whereas the notion of doctrinal development is now popular, such was not the case in the nineteenth century and earlier. There had been, of course, rudimentary statements regarding the development of doctrine, but nothing substantial until John Henry Newman produced *An Essay on the Development of Christian Doctrine*. Even though the theory of doctrinal development was not original with Newman, he treated it with such depth and with so many striking illustrations and presented his conclusions with such force that the work appears to the reader as an original creation.[1]

The significance of Newman in the formation of the mind of contemporary Catholicism can hardly be overestimated. Somewhat eclipsed during his lifetime, the star of the dead Newman began to shine brightly during the early part of this century. His genius first came to be recognized in Europe and was proclaimed by such men as Ambrose Gardiel, O.P., Henri Bremond, Francisco Marin-Sola, O.P., and Eric Pryzwara, S.J. By 1940, says Gustave Weigel, the pre-eminence of Newman as a theologian was universally accepted.[2] Jean Guitton thinks Newman should be given the title of Father of the Church, inasmuch as he adopted in advance the Church's mind of the future, as was characteristic of other great men who have received this title. Singlehandedly, Newman wrestled with the doctrines of such giants as Fichte, Feuerbach, Spencer, Hegel, Karl Marx, David Strauss, and Ernest Renan. The struggle produced a genius. Said Guitton: "What he wrote of St. Augustine is equally true of himself: 'He, noninfallible teacher, has formed the intellect of Christian Europe.'"[3]

An elaborate discussion of Newman's thought on doctrinal development is not necessary, but a brief comment is in order. The germinal ideas for his *Essay on Development* were first presented in the sermons he delivered at Oxford. One of these Oxford sermons, given in 1843, was entitled "The Theory of Developments in Religious Doctrine." It contained the notion that the Church in developing her doctrine is like Mary contemplating what has been revealed to her. As she meditates on what is given to her in faith, she develops a deeper understanding. Unlike Zachary, who balked at the angel's message,

[1] Joseph J. Reilley, "The Present Significance of Newman," *Thought,* XX (Spring, 1945), 390.
[2] John Henry Newman, *An Essay on the Development of Christian Doctrine,* introd. Gustave Weigel, S.J. (New York: Doubleday, 1960), p. 15.
[3] "Newman as a Modern Father of the Church," *Tablet,* CCXVIII (July 18, 1964), 814.

Mary received the word of God eagerly. But it was not enough
for Mary simply to acquiesce in providential happenings and
special revelations. She pondered the meaning of them. This
can be seen in Mary's response at the time of Jesus' birth
when the shepherds related what they had been told and at the
temple when the young Jesus proclaimed that he was about
his Father's business. In both cases Mary kept the events and
sayings in mind and pondered the meaning of them. Then,
at the wedding feast at Cana, when her understanding of
Jesus had increased considerably, Mary anticipated his first
miracle, telling the servants to do whatever he said to do.
Thus, Mary symbolizes the faith of both the unlearned who
receive the revelation of God in simple readiness and the
doctors who weigh and define what has been revealed. Thus,
Mary also symbolizes the evolutionary process by which the
whole Church develops what it has received in faith.[4]

In the same sermon, Newman depicts the development of a
dogma from its initial state of disorder to its final determina-
tion. Like a living force, the doctrinal idea takes hold of a
thousand minds, not to be contained or controlled. It erupts
like the burning fire shut up within the prophet until he can
no longer repress his utterances. It grows in the minds of
Christians through successive generations and is finally born.
In a way, it seems to use the minds of the Christians, rather
than being used by them. How wonderful it is, says Newman,
to trace the general course of a doctrine's development through
countless swayings back and forth, through reverses, inter-
ruptions, and hesitations to its ultimate completion, when each
part is in harmony and an emphatic unity is evident.[5]

The *Essay on Development* was published in 1845. It proved
to be a work of lasting value, as is evident from the tribute
paid to it by virtually all Catholics who have written on
this subject. In this lengthy work Newman suggests that the
ideas of faith follow the same pattern of development as the

---

[4] John Henry Newman, *Fifteen Sermons Preached before the University
of Oxford* (London: Longmans, Greene and Co., 1898), pp. 312–316.
[5] *Ibid.*

ideas of reason. But he recognizes the difficulty of establishing by the accumulation of historical evidence the continuity of an idea that transcends reason, as do the ideas of faith. For the evidence of history cannot always distinguish between what is revealed and what is not, what is development and what is corruption. To overcome this difficulty, Newman uses the method of setting up a hypothesis and testing it. Supposing that the Church today is the outgrowth of the early Church, what could be expected to have happened to its doctrines? In answering this question Newman sets up criteria by which an idea received in faith can be recognized in history. These criteria serve as notes which distinguish a development from a corruption. Specifically, these notes are as follows: (1) The doctrine preserves its original type or character. (2) There is a continuity of its principles. (3) It has a power of assimilation. (4) It has a logical sequence. (5) It anticipates its future. (6) It conserves its essential past. (7) It possesses a chronic vigor. By applying the above notes (or criteria) to a variety of doctrines, Newman establishes that development of doctrine does in fact occur.

Newman's theory of doctrinal development, set forth in succinct form, is that increase, expansion, and variation are necessary concommitants of

> any philosophy or polity which takes possession of the intellect and heart, and has any wide or extended dominion; that, from the nature of the human mind, time is necessary for the full comprehension and perfection of great ideas; and that the highest and most wonderful truths, though communicated to the world once for all by inspired teachers, could not be comprehended all at once by the recipients, but, as being received and transmitted by minds not inspired and through media which were human, have required only the longer time and deeper thought for their full elucidation.[6]

The validity of the principle of doctrinal development was definitively established by the Second Vatican Council. According to John Courtney Murray, S.J., chief architect of the Declaration on Religious Freedom, it was the idea of

---

[6] John Henry Newman, *An Essay on the Development of Christian Doctrine*, p. 53.

development, not the idea of religious freedom, that was the obstacle for those who opposed the Declaration to the end.[7] By finally adopting the Declaration in overwhelming numbers, the Council Fathers categorically committed themselves not only to religious freedom, but to the principle of doctrinal development as well. All the documents of Vatican II were influenced by the principle of doctrinal development. A few examples will suffice to show this influence. The Dogmatic Constitution on Divine Revelation says: "This tradition which comes from the apostles develops in the Church with the help of the Holy Spirit. For there is growth in the understanding of the realities and the words which have been handed down" (n. 8).[8] Again, the same document says: "The Church is concerned to move ahead daily toward a deeper understanding of sacred Scriptures" (n. 23).[9] The Dogmatic Constitution on the Church states: "The Church becomes on earth the budding form of that future kingdom. While she slowly grows, the Church strains toward the consummation of the Kingdom" (n. 5).[10] The Constitution on the Church in the Modern World treats the principle of development as a vital force in the community of man: "The human race has passed from a rather static concept of reality to a more dynamic, evolutionary one" (n. 5).[11]

The thinking of the Council Fathers on the notion of doctrinal development had been conditioned by contemporary theologians who were strongly influenced by Newman. Many of these theologians have written at length on the subject of doctrinal development, adding deeper insights. Karl Rahner, S.J., for example, says that the theory of doctrinal development explains the process by which the Church defines propositions as divinely revealed which were not always taught as revealed, or which restate the substance of a belief already defined in radically different terms, or which cannot be proved

7 Abbott, *op. cit.*, p. 673.
8 *Ibid.*, p. 116.
9 *Ibid.*, p. 126.
10 *Ibid.*, p. 18.
11 *Ibid.*, p. 204.

empirically to date back to the apostles.[12] In discussing the problems surrounding the doctrine of the bodily assumption of Mary, Rahner relates that this doctrine did not find expression in an explicit statement until the papal definition was issued in 1950. Today we are able to grasp its identity with its earlier expressions. But it was not proposed in every age with the same clarity, precision, and force that characterize it today. Therefore, the doctrine of the assumption has, "in a sense still to be determined, 'come to be,' within the course of human history, for when the Gospel was first preached this doctrine was not found in its present form."[13]

A certain reserve, maintains Edward Schillebeeckx, O.P., must accompany one's assent to dogma; there is always a danger that assent will reach beyond the substance of dogma and fasten on the form in which it is expressed. Doctrine continues to develop, even after it is defined. However, before a development occurs, it is in no way apparent which part of a teaching constitutes the essence and which part the trappings. Says Schillebeeckx: "In the initial period where no differentiation is made, the Church and all the faithful will speak almost as a matter of course as if the outward form were part of the very heart of dogma." Only when a specific question "is expressly raised by man's new experiences, or by new positive data, can it become apparent whether the so-called 'clothing' is but a mode of expression or really belongs to the dogmatic content." Furthermore, no proposition can fully contain the revelation it expresses: "In a dogma the religious mystery is expressed in human concepts which are never adequate to provide an exhaustive grasp of the mystery." Consequently, further refinement is always possible.[14]

According to Herbert Hammans, a general *theory* of doc-

---

[12] Karl Rahner, S.J., and Herbert Vorgrimler, S.J., *Theological Dictionary,* trans. Richard Strachan (New York: Herder and Herder, 1965); pp. 125–126.

[13] Karl Rahner, S.J., *Theological Investigations,* trans. Cornelius Ernst, O.P. (Baltimore: Helicon Press, 1961), I, 39.

[14] Edward H. Schillebeeckx, O.P., "The Concept of Truth and Related Problems," *Ecumenism and the Roman Catholic Church,* ed. Leo Alting von Geusau, trans. H. J. J. Vaughan, J. S. Harding and the Documentation Centre (Westminster, Maryland: The Newman Press, 1966), pp. 164–165.

trinal development may explain certain doctrinal changes, but no *law* of developments can be deduced from the changes. Each doctrine proceeds along a course of development proper to its own inner laws and dynamism. Hammans says that the history of dogma contains many surprises. Like all historical developments, the development of dogma is unique. It cannot be reduced to a system of unchanging principles or laws. Nor can it be challenged by invoking such principles or laws. "We should constantly remember," says Hammans, "that a complete theory of development is possible when the development of dogma is finished, and for us that means, in fact, never."[15] The editors of the *Catholic Mind* put it this way: "Theology . . . formulates ways of expressing as accurately as possible a truth given once and for all." But when new circumstances bring new insights, a particular doctrine "develops in accordance with its own inner laws."[16]

Doctrinal development must not be viewed as arising spontaneously and exclusively from sources within the Church. It frequently happens that external influences play the key role in doctrinal development. Developments in the secular order tend to induce similar developments in the Church. The division between the Church and the world is not as sharply defined as essentialists might like to believe. Schillebeeckx says that in some areas the Church and the world cannot be distinguished: "Within the inviolable limits set by the Word, the sacrament, and the office—and all those forms of service— the boundaries between the Church and mankind are blurred."[17] In many ways, the Church has become what the world has made it. According to Schillebeeckx, "there is obviously going on throughout mankind a process of bringing things into the Church."[18]

15 Herbert Hammans, "Recent Catholic Views on the Development of Dogma," *Man as Man and Believer,* ed. Edward Schillebeeckx, O.P., Vol. XXI of *Concilium,* ed. Edward Schillebeeckx, O.P., *et al.* (New York: Paulist Press, 1967), p. 112.
16 "Development of Doctrine," *Catholic Mind,* LXI (November, 1963), 3.
17 Edward H. Schillebeeckx, O.P. (ed.), *The Church and Mankind,* Vol. I of *Concilium,* ed. Edward H. Schillebeeckx, O.P., *et al.* (New York; Paulist Press, 1965), p. 99.
18 *Ibid.*

A case in point is the principle of doctrinal development itself. Even though Newman's *Essay on Development* preceded publication of Darwin's thought on organic evolution, the idea was already around, says Gustave Weigel.[19] Furthermore, Newman was not yet a Catholic when he wrote all but a small portion of the *Essay on Development*. After Newman entered the Catholic Church, he was unable to procure an imprimatur from Cardinal Wiseman, but he took Wiseman's suggestion and had the work published as the thought of an Anglican.[20] A century later there was still entrenched opposition within Roman Catholicism to the notion of development.

The influence of external forces in the development of Church doctrine can also be seen in the case of Teilhard de Chardin. The initial resistance by Church authorities to his thought is well known. Pained by the censorship that was imposed upon him, Chardin suffered quietly and continued writing, not knowing when, if ever, his works might be published. Belatedly recognized by Church authorities, Chardin's thought has now permeated Catholic consciousness. From the world of science, Chardin has introduced fascinating visions and exciting possibilities. In all of his thinking, the evolution of man is basic. Because of his insights, Roman Catholic theologians are even more firmly convinced of the validity of the principle of doctrinal development. A few lines from Chardin will not only convey the late paleontologist's insight into evolution, but they will also provide an understanding of a strong current in the stream of contemporary Catholic thought:

> For a long time, it was still possible for us to believe that the increasing aggregation of mankind was nothing more than a superficial arrangement of the human units in the search for a more comfortable life.
> But today, as a result of a better survey of Time and Space, another idea is about to dawn in our mind. Namely, we begin to realize that, under the veil of human socialization, there may be the same basic and universal force operating which, since the dawn of the world, has constantly striven towards an ever-growing organization

19 Newman, *An Essay on The Development of Christian Doctrine*, p. 11.
20 *Ibid.*, p. 14.

of Matter. We must no longer think of this force as a mere spatial motion of the Earth (Galileo), but as the tightening beyond ourselves and above our heads, of a sort of cosmic vortex, which, after generating each one of us individually, pushes further through the building of collective units, on its steady course towards a continuous and simultaneous increase of complexity and consciousness.[21]

The findings of sociology and biology have also helped Catholics to recognize the validity of the principle of doctrinal development. Francois Houtart writes about the developments in the modern world which make possible both personal growth and personal deformity. We are in a radically different environment today. Houtart is quite emphatic about this: "The fact is that we *are* in a new world, one which is requiring new thought, new adaptation, new action, new institutions from us continuously." We know a lot more about men, biologically and socially. Each molecule or atom of living matter has a particular code enabling an organism, say, the human body, to develop a certain way. If we could decifer this code and change it, the same molecules or atoms would produce something else.[22] We might, for example, be able to program into the human body a code that would effect the renewal of aging tissue, or that would effect the growth of new limbs to replace ones that have been severed, or that would repair damage done to vital organs like the heart. With each new discovery that helps to overcome the limitations of nature, new theological considerations arise. As developments in secular thought occur, corresponding developments in religious thought may be expected.

Further evidence that developments in the world have helped establish the principle of doctrinal development within the Church may be found in the influences that have altered the classical notion of natural law. Modern insights into the evolutionary nature of man have spilled over into Catholic

---

[21] Teilhard de Chardin, S.J., "The Psychological Conditions of Human Unification," *Cross Currents*, III (Fall, 1952), 1, 4–5.
[22] Francois Houtart, *The Challenge to Change*, ed. Mary Anne Chouteau (New York: Sheed and Ward, 1964), pp. 65–66.

thinking on natural law, a sturdy pillar in the structure of Catholic teaching. Speaking the mind of a great number of theologians, Gregory Baum, O.S.A., argues for an evolutionary understanding of natural law. He says that he has difficulty, not only with the way the concept was understood in the past, but with the concept itself. He gives two reasons for his difficulty with the phrase "natural law." The first difficulty is that the concept suggests a rigid set of formulated laws, but "there will never be any ultimate formulation of the natural." The natural law must be viewed simply as the "deep inclination of man to be faithful to himself, the orientation of man to grow and mature, to seek truth and to do good." The second difficulty is with the word "natural"—it is ambiguous. "Grace, as call, is active everywhere! We have no way of knowing whether a moral conviction which matures in the consciences of men is simply natural, or whether it is not the work of redemptive grace in them." Therefore, Baum concludes, while "I affirm the reality called 'natural law,' it seems to me that this is neither natural nor is it law." He finds confirmation of his interpretation of natural law in *Pacem in Terris*. In this encyclical Pope John anchors the thing he calls "natural law," not in man's nature, but in his person. "Central in Pope John's thought," says Baum, "is the person. It is the person of man which we discover as unique and precious, to which correspond certain rights and duties as an expression of his dignity."[23]

Supporting the idea that the natural law theory has been influenced and perfected by forces external to the Catholic Church is an article by Raymond J. Nogar, O.P., on "The Emergence of the Person in Natural Law Theory." Nogar explains that the concept of interpersonalism "asserts that the proximate specific root of human right is the deliberate, reciprocal interrelationship of free, intelligent men in the concrete social situation." The flourishing of interpersonalism in

---

[23] Gregory Baum, O.S.A., "The Christian Adventure: Risk and Renewal," *Furrow*, XVI (June, 1965), 344–346.

natural law theory is due, says Nogar, to the dialogue between natural law theorists and proponents of *non-transcendent* varieties of evolution, historicism, and existentialism. Each of these theories, in effect, denies the existence of a transcendent, personal God. The greatest foes of natural law ever to arise in history, these theories forced the defenders of natural law to re-examine their position. The result was a pruning away of some of the untenable explanations of natural law and a grafting in of the common insight of these three theories, namely, the insight that "if man's emergence and unique development has a direction, . . . it is toward greater freedom, creativity, and personal realization."[24]

One can detect in Nogar's essay the thought of Martin Buber, whose writings in the area of interpersonal relations are ubiquitously quoted. Among his more pertinent works on this subject are *I and Thou, Between Man and Man,* and *The Knowledge of Man.* But only recently have his works had a large Catholic audience. This is another example of how the development of doctrine is dependent upon external stimuli.

The history of the Roman Catholic Church is replete with instances of the adoption of the thought and practice of the secular order and of other religious bodies. The most recent instance of this is seen in the manner in which the doctrine of religious freedom developed. There is an immense difference between the attitudes that generated the Inquisition and those that embraced the notion of religious freedom. Catholics admit, finally, that the Inquisition cannot be justified by the Gospel. What post-Vatican II Catholicism understands by the notion of religious freedom certainly was not in evidence within the Church to any appreciable degree in recent centuries. Clearly, a change has occurred. According to John Courtney Murray, S.J., it is the principle of doctrinal development that makes possible our present understanding of religious freedom. This new insight into religious freedom stems

---

[24] Raymond J. Nogar, O.P., "The Emergence of the Person in Natural Law Theory," *Chicago Studies,* V (Spring, 1966), 84–86.

from the "theological position in which the dignity of the human person has emerged more clearly and centrally."[25] There can be no doubt that this development within Catholicism is dependent upon external influences, particularly those in the United States. Protestants, Jews, secular humanists, and others have all contributed to the development of the religious freedom that characterizes pluralistic America. It was not by accident that the bishops of the United States came into their own at the Second Vatican Council when the question of religious liberty was debated. The bishops of the United States had been conditioned by their environment. Nor was it an accident that the chief architect of the document on religious freedom was the American Jesuit, John Courtney Murray. Said Murray: "The issue of religious liberty is of the highest interest to me both as a theologian and as an American. It is, as it were, *the* American issue at the council."[26]

Clearly, the principle of doctrinal development is inherent in Catholic thought. Clearly, also, development often results from the influence of external forces. Now, because doctrine develops, a democratic form of government in the Church seems to be *possible*. If the principle of doctrinal development can explain, as Murray says it does, the difference between the Syllabus of Errors in 1864 and the Declaration on Religious Freedom in 1965,[27] the same principle can explain the transformation of Church government from the present monarchical form to a future democratic form. And because the occasion for development of doctrine is often the influence of external forces, a democratic form of Church government seems to be *desirable*. For monarchical structures, resistant to change, often facilitate doctrinal lags and the suppression

---

25 John Courtney Murray, S.J., "Religious Liberty and Development of Doctrine," interview by Edward Gaffney, *Catholic World,* CCIV (February, 1967), 276.
26 Eugene K. Culhane, S.J. (ed.), *American Catholic Horizons* (New York: Doubleday & Company, 1966), p. 219.
27 John Courtney Murray, S. J., "Introduction" [to the Declaration on Religious Freedom], *The Documents of Vatican II,* ed. Walter M. Abbott, S.J. (New York: Guild Press, 1965), p. 673.

of men like Newman and Chardin. In a democracy, however, the leaders more readily absorb the new ideas that take hold among the people. It is the ability of the leaders to respond to the thought of the people that enables them to remain in office.

CHAPTER IV

THE PEOPLE OF GOD

An objection frequently raised against a democratic form of Church government is that the laity would lead the Church astray. The argument runs something like this. Truth cannot be determined by majority vote. Jesus established a hierarchy as an infallible guide in matters of revealed truth. Therefore, it is not the will of the laity but the will of the hierarchy that must prevail. The answer to this argument is found in the concept of the People of God. Chief among the characteristics of the People of God are these: freedom, infallibility, fidelity, and equality. An examination of each of these characteristics will show that revealed truth is more apt to be served if the Church is a democracy than if it is a monarchy.

First, let us examine the characteristic of freedom. Whereas both truth and freedom are important, freedom has a priority. Ultimately, when the parousia arrives, there will be no conflict between truth and freedom. In the meantime, however, there will be conflicts. And whereas God desires that the truth be known, he does not want this at the expense of freedom. When truth and freedom seem to conflict in particular situations, it is freedom which should take precedence over truth. This is true not only because man is free by nature and by grace, but also because freedom is a necessary matrix for the proper development of truth.

It may be helpful at this point to draw a lesson from a

Rabbinic story. On a certain occasion, as the story goes, Rabbi Eliezer found himself in disagreement with his fellow Rabbis. After exhausting every conceivable argument to prove his point, he was still unable to convince his colleagues. Therefore, as a last resort, he invoked the miraculous power of God. If I am correct, he said, let that tree move a hundred yards. And it did. The other Rabbis replied that nothing can be proved by a tree. So, he said, let it be proved by the canal. And the water in the canal reversed its course. They replied that nothing can be proved by water. So, he said, let the walls of this house prove it. And they began to bend inwards as if to collapse. But another Rabbi, Josua, rebuked the walls, saying that a Rabbinic debate was none of their business. And so out of respect for Rabbi Josua they did not collapse, but out of respect for Rabbi Eliezer they did not return all the way to their original position. Then a voice from heaven spoke out, asking the group what they had against Rabbi Eliezer, who is always right. Rabbi Josua replied that it was the revelation given at Sinai that was to be followed, not a voice from heaven. And the revelation at Sinai was that decisions are to be made by a majority ("Exodus XXIII homiletically interpreted"). Later, one of the Rabbis met Elijah and asked him what God had done when he was faced with Rabbi Josua's squelching remark. Elijah replied that God had laughed and said that his children had conquered him.[1]

Now, the lesson to be learned from this story is that in concrete situations, when there is a conflict between truth and freedom, freedom has priority. This is true even in situations involving Church government. If such were not the case, the pope and bishops would never have been allowed by God to make bad decisions in exercising their jurisdictional power. But as history and present experience testify, they have made many mistakes. God has granted them this freedom even though in the short term truth has suffered. The laws of cen-

---

[1] C. G. Montefiore and H. Lowe, *A Rabbinic Anthology* (London: Macmillan and Co., Ltd., 1930), pp. 340–341.

sorship, for example, seem to have done more to obscure truth than to promote it. Chardin's contributions would perhaps have been immeasurably greater had it not been for censorship. For then his thought would have been subject to the criticism of other great minds. Challenged, Chardin's genius would have provided even greater insights. God allows the Church to be free, even if it imposes absurd restrictions upon itself, even if truth suffers, as it did in Chardin's case. Other mistakes can be cited: the suppression of Father Ricci in China, the excommunication of Martin Luther (though many disagree), the mishandling of the Gallileo situation, the support of the Inquisition, and so forth. Now, if God allows freedom to prevail over truth in a monarchical form of Church government, monarchy cannot be defended on the grounds that it is a better instrument than democracy in guiding people. In both monarchy and democracy, the rulers make mistakes detrimental to truth. In a democracy, however, the rulers who obstruct the development of truth can more easily be removed from office.

At this point a distinction between teaching and jurisdictional authority is in order. According to the *Catholic Encyclopedia* there is an essential difference between these two types of authority. They have different objects. Teaching authority "is concerned solely with the manifestation of revealed doctrine; the object of the power of jurisdiction is to establish and enforce such laws and regulations as are necessary to the well-being of the Church."[2] It is clear from the definition of the First Vatican Council that "infallibility (whether of the Church at large or of the pope) is affirmed only in regard to doctrine."[3]

The Church is simply not preserved from mistakes in jurisdiction. According to Alois Muller, even the worst law could not have the same detrimental effect as the denial of a dogma.

[2] William H. W. Fanning, "The Church," *Catholic Encyclopedia* (New York: The Encyclopedia Press, 1913), III, 755.
[3] P. J. Tonner, "Infallibility," *Catholic Encyclopedia* (New York: The Encyclopedia Press, 1913), VII, 799.

Contrary to opinions of some Churchmen, says Muller, the Holy Spirit does not protect the Church against jurisdictional decisions that would do grave damage to the Church. History shows that the Holy Spirit may remain ineffective even in matters of utmost importance. "We may give as possible examples," continues Muller, "the attitude of Humbert de Silva Candida in Constantinople in 1054 which led to the schism; all the opportunities for reform which were missed in the fifteenth century and at the beginning of the sixteenth; the controversy about rites and its result in the eighteenth century; and the policy concerning the States of the Church in the nineteenth century."[4] These serious mistakes are possible because the Church and the pope have the same weaknesses that impair secular governments. In short and in the words of John Henry Newman, "a pope is not infallible in his laws, nor in his commands, nor in his acts of state, nor in his administration, nor in his public policy."[5]

Actually, the question of infallibility is somewhat irrelevant to the issue of democracy versus monarchy. It is the pope as *teacher* who receives the charism of infallibility, not the pope as *ruler*. A pope elected in a democratic Church would be protected by the same charism of infallibility that would protect a papal monarch as teacher. Dogmas could be defined and truth could be served just as easily in a democratic Church where a new pope is elected every few years as in a monarchy where an aging pope clings to the chair of Peter through various stages of senility until the angel of death finally removes him from office.

Now, let us consider the second characteristic of the People of God, namely, infallibility. The People of God as a whole is infallible. This is clear from a variety of sources. The *Catholic Encyclopedia* quotes the First Vatican Council, which declared that "the doctrine of faith, which God has revealed, . . . has been committed as a Divine deposit to the

---

4 Alois Muller, *Obedience in the Church,* trans. Hilda Graef (Westminster, Maryland: The Newman Press, 1966), pp. 69–72.
5 John Henry Newman, *A Letter Addressed to His Grace the Duke of Norfolk* (London: B. M. Pickering, 1875), p. 62.

spouse of Christ,"[6] that is, to the Church, not just to the pope. "The infallibility claimed for the pope is the same in its nature, scope and extent as that which the Church as a whole possesses," according to the *Catholic Encyclopedia*.[7] Even prior to the First Vatican Council, Cardinal Newman had said that the faithful's *"consensus* through Christendom is the voice of the Infallible Church."[8] The Second Vatican Council makes the same point in the Constitution on the Church: "The body of the faithful as a whole, anointed as they are by the Holy One (cf. Jn. 2:20,27), cannot err in matters of belief" (n. 12).[9]

There is much confusion today over the concept of infallibity. Some of the confusion arises when the concept is understood too broadly, and some arises when it is understood too narrowly. The common understanding of infallibility is that when the pope speaks as head of the Church on faith and morals he cannot err. This is understood too broadly when "faith and morals" is interpreted to mean more than the deposit of revealed truth. It is understood too narrowly when it is interpreted as belonging exclusively to the pope and not to the whole Church as well.

As to the first misconception (which interprets infallibility too broadly), Gregory Baum writes:

> It is important to understand what ecclesiastical documents mean by the expression "teaching on faith and morals." By a common misunderstanding "faith" here refers to divine revelation and "morals" to the whole field of the moral life. In reality, however, "the teaching on faith and morals" refers to divine revelation.
>
> The *Constitution on the Church* circumscribes the area in which the Church is called to exercise her infallible teaching: it "extends as far as the deposit of revelation extends, which must be religiously guarded and faithfully expounded." . . .[10]

---

[6] P. J. Tonner, *op. cit.*, pp. 790–791.
[7] *Ibid.*, p. 796.
[8] John Henry Newman, "On Consulting the Faithful in Matters of Doctrine," *Cross Currents*, II (Summer, 1952), 72.
[9] Abbott, *op. cit.*, p. 29.
[10] Gregory Baum, O.S.A., "Teaching Authority of Vatican II," *Ecumenist*, III (September-October, 1965), 89–92.

The second misconception (which interprets infallibility too narrowly) sees the pope as someone over and apart from the Church and not as one who shares the gifts in common (even if uniquely) with the whole People of God. It sees the charism of infallibility being located primarily in the papacy and secondarily in the Church. But the Church is not infallible because the pope is infallible. Just the reverse is true. If infallibility were not primarily a charism of the whole Church and only secondarily a charism of the pope, the purpose of infallibility could not be achieved, namely, the distinguishing between what is of revelation and what is not in such a way that it can be known with complete certitude by the faithful. Inasmuch as the pope can be mistaken on matters that are not revealed, the faithful are incapable of knowing through reason whether a given proposition arises from faith or from fancy. The faithful know the difference between a statement that *is* infallible and one that is *not* only because they already possess the full deposit of faith without error, i.e., infallibly. Without this prior infallibility on the part of the faithful, there would be no way for them to be certain of the validity of a proposition presented as infallible. Whether a proposition is infallible or not is in no way open to rational demonstration. It begs the question to say that the pope is speaking as head of the Church. This can be known only if the whole deposit of faith is already perceived without error, infallibly, by the faithful.

Now, if the People of God as a whole is infallible, there is no more to fear from democracy than from monarchy. A pope in a democratic Church would be just as infallible as a pope in a monarchical Church. The same holds true for the faithful. Individual laymen may cut themselves off from dogma, as may individual bishops, but the faithful as a whole will remain loyal. For it is not the form of government that produces infallibility and unity, but the Holy Spirit. In short, because the whole People of God is infallible, a democratic Church is possible.

We are now ready to consider the third characteristic of

the People of God—fidelity. The People of God are a faithful people. As such, they preserve the revelation that has been given to the Church in faith. Therefore, the magisterium (teaching authority) has the responsibility of *consulting the faithful* in the process of developing doctrine. This of course necessitates communication, which is far more easily achieved in the dialogical situations characteristic of democracy than in the monological situations characteristic of monarchy.

Though the idea of consulting the faithful is widely accepted now, it seemed quite radical in Newman's time. This was evident from the reaction which followed the publication of his essay, "On Consulting the Faithful in Matters of Doctrine." This essay created such a panic in England and Rome that he stopped writing for five years. According to John Coulson, the appearance of this essay did irreparable harm to Newman's career within the Church. It gained for him the Pope's extreme displeasure, a charge of heresy by the Bishop of Newport, and the reputation of being "the most dangerous man in England."[11] Although the essay originally appeared in the *Rambler* during Newman's lifetime, it was not published in book form until 1962. Gary Wills attributes this to the conservative influence of William Ward, nineteenth century editor of the *Dublin Review,* and Father Fenton, twentieth century editor of the *American Ecclesiastical Review.*[12] When it finally appeared in book form, it struck the contemporary theological scene "like a two-edged sword."[13] It was the very thing laymen needed to make them begin asserting their rights more forcefully.[14]

---

[11] Oona Sullivan, Review of *On Consulting the Faithful in Matters of Doctrine,* by John Henry Newman, ed. John Coulson, *Jubilee,* IX (March, 1963), 51.

[12] Gary Wills, "The Most Dangerous Man," *National Review,* XIII (October, 23, 1967), 320.

[13] Philip C. Rule, S.J., Review of *On Consulting the Faithful in Matters of Doctrine,* by John Henry Newman, ed. John Coulson, *Review for Religious,* XXI (September, 1962), 472.

[14] Charles Palms, C.S.P., Review of *On Consulting the Faithful in Matters of Doctrine,* by John Henry Newman, ed. John Coulson, *Catholic World,* CICVI (February, 1963), 317.

In his now famous essay, Newman asks why the faithful "are treated by the Holy See" on certain occasions involving doctrine "with such attention and consideration." The answer, says Newman, is that "the body of the faithful is one of the witnesses of the fact of tradition or revealed doctrine, and because their *consensus* through Christendom is the voice of the Infallible Church."[15] Newman goes on to explain how the consensus of the faithful manifests the tradition of the Church: (1) by testifying to apostolic revelation, (2) by being a kind of instinct in the body of Christ, (3) by responding to the direction of the Holy Spirit, (4) by answering to prayer, and (5) by being scandalized by error.[16]

Newman selected the period of the Arian heresy as the historical basis for his argument. The Council of Nicaea in A.D. 325 had declared that the Son was consubstantial with the Father. This the Arians denied, as did, according to Newman, the vast majority of scholars and bishops. His argument develops as follows. Even though the fourth century was the age of doctors—Athanasius, Hilary, the two Gregories, Basil, Chrysostom, Ambrose, Jerome, and Augustine—"the divine tradition was proclaimed and maintained far more by the faithful than by the Episcopate." Newman sees in the history of Arianism a prime example of a case in which it was necessary to go to the faithful in order to discover the apostolic tradition. The bishops and doctors debated among themselves and confused their readers. But the consensus of the faithful rang loud and clear. The voice of the faithful, then, was the voice of tradition during the period of the Arian heresy. Even greater certainty of this comes with the realization that the doctrine in question was the foundation of the Christian system, that the controversy lasted sixty years, and that the faithful suffered property loss, injury, and even death in preserving their apostolic belief.[17]

---

15 John Henry Newman, "On Consulting the Faithful in Matters of Doctrine," 74.
16 *Ibid.*, 81.
17 *Ibid.*, 82–83.

Newman then proceeds to document his case with historical evidence. He establishes conclusively that the Nicene dogma was preserved, "not by the unwavering firmness of the Holy See, Councils, or Bishops," but by the consensus of the faithful. The historical evidence Newman presents is simply overpowering. Twenty-two indictments are brought against the teaching Church, each one revealing quite clearly that the official teachers were either badly confused or in violent opposition.[18] The twenty-two instances establish beyond a reasonable doubt what the charitable and soft-spoken Newman must in all honesty proclaim:

> The body of Bishops failed in their confession of the faith. They spoke variously, one against another; there was nothing, after Nicaea, of firm, unvarying, consistent testimony, for nearly sixty years. There were untrustworthy Councils, unfaithful Bishops; there was weakness, fear of consequences, misguidance, delusion, hallucination, endless, hopeless, extending itself into nearly every corner of the Catholic Church. The comparatively few who remained faithful were discredited and driven into exile; the rest were either deceivers or were deceived.[19]

After revealing the perfidy of the hierarchy, Newman demonstrates the "fidelity of the laity." He cites twenty-one instances of their fidelity, drawing testimony from Alexandria, Constantinople, Syria, Cappadocia, Antioch, Edessa, Samosats, Osroene, Pontus, Armenia, Nicomedia, Asia Minor, Scytha, Illyria, the neighborhood of Macedonia, Rome, Milan, and Christendom generally. In Alexandria, for example, the Arian bishops waged a persecution against all the faithful. As related by Athanasius, whom Newman quotes, the Arian bishops gathered a great number of herdsmen, shepherds, and dissolute youths and ran rampant over the faithful, whom they killed, trampled under foot, beat with the whip, cast into prison, dragged away by the hair, raped, and starved. All this was done "for no other reason but that they might be induced to join the Arians, and receive Gregory."[20]

18 *Ibid.*, 83–84.
19 *Ibid.*, 83.
20 *Ibid.*, 27.

From what Newman has written it is abundantly clear that the consensus of the faithful is the voice of tradition and that it should be listened to by the hierarchy. Newman's position has wide acceptance today. According to Michael Novak, Newman's thought exerted a profound influence on the Second Vatican Council. His ideas had so penetrated Catholicism that many bishops were expounding them without being aware of their origin. Novak illustrates this point by quoting and paraphrasing the talk given by Pedro Cantero Guadrado of Huelva, Spain: "The 'instinct of faith' is a gift from the Spirit, given to all members of the People of God, collectively and individually. It works as an 'instinct for truth' on questions of faith and morals." Developing the thought further, Novak then concludes by saying: "Thus the great vision of John Henry Newman entered the Council through a Spanish bishop who, perhaps, had never read him."[21]

The necessity of consulting the faithful in matters of doctrine is proclaimed today by such progressive thinkers as John L. McKenzie, S.J., and Karl Rahner, S.J. McKenzie says that not only the officers but all the members of the Church make decisions on faith. This is why one of the faithful can sometimes see when a decision by an officer is not based on faith. It is not necessary that a person have an intimate knowledge of the situation before recognizing that the faith is being compromised by a decision of an officer. When a person is less involved and has less at stake, he is often more objective and sometimes possesses an insight which the officers do not have. Says McKenzie, "authority can protect itself against decisions made without faith by consulting the Church."[22] The words of Karl Rahner, S.J., contain the same notion:

Although the learning Church believes as instructed by the magisterium and on this score is infallible as a whole, yet the believing Church can and must be consulted by the magisterium (D1836) because the latter's judgment is based on tradition, which cannot

21 Novak, *The Open Church*, p. 153.
22 McKenzie, *Authority in the Church*, pp. 179–180.

possibly be ascertained without reference to the faith of the Church, not merely her doctrine.[23]

Because the magisterium should consult the faithful in matters of doctrine, a system of good communication is necessary within the Church. In a monarchy, communication stops if a Church officer closes his ears. But in a democracy communication can be reopened through elective processes. A new officer can be voted in. The threat of being removed from office is a healthy safeguard against the lack of communication which now characterizes the monarchical form of Church government. If doctrine is to develop with enough speed to keep abreast of the new situations that arise so frequently in this accelerated age, a more flexible and responsive form of government is needed. In short, the time has arrived when it is fitting that democracy be incorporated into the Church.

The fourth characteristic mentioned at the beginning of this chapter may now be discussed, namely, the *equality* of the people of God. The People of God all share a fundamental equality. The monarchical form of government, however, prevents this fundamental equality from being adequately manifested. Having been accustomed to monarchy for so long, many Catholics have come to visualize the Church as a pyramid. But the pyramidal image is not compatible with scripture or with the notion that the People of God share a fundamental equality. Let us therefore examine the reasons why the pyramidal image of the Church should be rejected and then discuss the equality of the People of God in some detail.

The notion of the Church as the People of God counteracts the image of the Church as a pyramid. The pyramidal image suggests the following line of thought. The top stone is the pope. Next comes the layer of stones made up of bishops. Next the layer made up of priests. Then the layer made up of religious. And finally the bottom layer made up of the laity, who support the rest of the structure. The pope is up

---

[23] Rahner, *Theological Dictionary,* p. 269.

high close to God, who conveys truths and directives through the pope, who in turn passes them down through the bishops to the priests, religious, and laity. All initiative comes from the top. Those underneath are to believe and obey. But this image is unscriptural. If the Church must be viewed as a structure, the following image is much more consistent with scripture and with the notion that the People of God are equal. Jesus said he would build his Church *on* Peter, not under him. Jesus is the chief foundation stone. And Peter (the pope) is supposed to remain close to Jesus at the bottom of the structure, a support to the brethren. The Church consists of living stones that are being built up into a spiritual house. The foundation stones are the apostles (bishops) and prophets (who in some cases are laymen). The relationship the different members have in the structure depends primarily upon holiness, not upon office. The holier a person is, the closer he is to Christ, the closer he is to the bottom, for Christ is the chief foundation stone.

The Second Vatican Council repudiated the pyramidal image of the Church by describing it as a mystery. The Council drew on many images of scripture to help reveal the mystery of the Church. For example, in the Constitution on the Church, the Council uses the following images from scripture to describe the Church: a sheepfold, a flock, a tract of land, an olive tree, a vineyard, an edifice, a house, a temple, a city, a bride, a mother, an exile (n. 6).[24] These images, in effect, reject the non-biblical pyramidal image of the Church.

The pyramidal image of the Church was further rejected by the bishops when they proclaimed the fundamental equality of the members of the Church. The bishops took pains to spell out this fundamental equality in unmistakable language: "All share a true equality with regard to the dignity common to all the faithful" (Constitution on the Church, n. 32).[25] It was necessary, the bishops felt, to state that there is an essen-

---

[24] Abbott, *op. cit.*, pp. 18–20.
[25] *Ibid.*, p. 58.

tial difference between the priesthood of the laity and the ministerial priesthood. But in spite of this, the undeniable truth of the new creation remains—*all* share a "true equality": the pope, the bishops, the priests, the religious, and the laity. The bishops do not dispense rights and responsibilities; these flow from the relationship one has with Christ as brother and Lord. The pope receives his rights and responsibilities directly from Christ. But so do the bishops, the priests, and the laity. Says the Constitution on the Church: "The lay apostolate is a participation in the saving mission of the Church itself. Through their baptism and confirmation, all are commissioned to that apostolate by the Lord Himself" (n.33).[26] The gifts come from the Holy Spirit, who distributes to all: "There is only one Spirit who, according to His own richness and the needs of the ministers, distributes His different gifts for the welfare of the Church" (n. 7). Further, these gifts are given so that we may serve one another in love: "He continually distributes in His body, that is, in the Church, gifts of ministries through which, by His own power, we serve each other unto salvation, . . . carrying out the truth in love" (n. 7).[27] The principle that binds the People of God together is not force or domination or law, but love, that is, the Spirit himself: "Behold the days shall come, saith the Lord, and I will make a new covenant with the house of Israel, and with the house of Juda. . . . I will give my law in their bowels, and I will write it in their heart: and I will be their God, and they will be my people" (n. 9).[28]

Because the People of God share a fundamental equality, it is no longer permissible to view the priest as one who performs spiritual duties and the layman as one who performs temporal duties. Depending upon the gift of the Spirit, a layman or a priest is called to service in either the world or the Church or both. "The laity," say the bishops in the

---

[26] *Ibid.*, p. 59.
[27] *Ibid.*, p. 21.
[28] *Ibid.*, p. 25.

Decree on the Apostolate of the Laity, "derive the right and duty with respect to the apostolate from their union with Christ their Head" (n. 3). The Holy Spirit, "gives to the faithful special gifts as well (cf. 1 Cor. 12:7), 'allotting to everyone as he will' (cf. 1 Cor. 12:11)" (n. 3).[29]

The pyramidal image of the Church lent itself to a preoccupation with the administrative aspects of the Church. The understanding of the Church as the People of God, however, brings into focus the charismatic aspects of the Church. In a speech before the Council Fathers on "The Charismatic Dimension of the Church," Cardinal Leon Suenens spoke as follows: "To St. Paul the Church of the living Christ does not appear as some kind of administrative organization, but as a living web of gifts, of charisms, of ministries. The Spirit is given to every individual Christian, the Spirit who gives his gifts, his charisms, to each and every one."[30]

The belief in the Church as the People of God provides an excellent rationale for the democratization of the Roman Catholic Church. Because the Church is made up of free people who share a fundamental equality and who receive gifts directly from the Spirit, the structures ought to be such that this fundamental equality is adequately demonstrated. Democracy, it would seem, is more conducive to this end than monarchy. If the truth is to develop properly, opportunities for the conflict of opinion must be built into the system of government. Writing on the belief in conflict of opinions for the emergence of truth, Protestant historian Sidney Mead says that this belief,

> as Jefferson worded it in his "Act for Establishing Religious Freedom" in Virginia, was
>
>> that truth is great and will prevail if left to herself; that she is the proper and sufficient antagonist to error, and has nothing to fear from the conflict unless by human interposition disarmed of her

---

[29] *Ibid.*, p. 492.
[30] Hans Küng, Yves Congar, O.P., and Daniel O'Hanlon, S.J., *Council Speeches of Vatican II* (Glen Rock, New Jersey: Paulist Press, 1964), pp. 31–32.

natural weapon, free argument and debate; errors ceasing to be dangerous when it is permitted freely to contradict them.

The dimension of this belief that has tended to fade into limbo is the idea that the truth emerges "from the conflict" itself—that is, that in order for the truth to emerge at all conflict of opinions is essential.[31]

Monarchical structures do not lend themselves to a conflict of opinions and to a full exercise of inalienable rights, for they provide no means by which the collective will of the People of God is necessarily embraced by the hierarchy. Unless the People of God share in the decision making processes of the Church, their voice is not apt to be heard. Nor are they likely to feel disposed to express themselves, knowing that their words may have little effect. Monarchical structures lend themselves to the preservation of a paternalism which obscures the fundamental equality of the People of God. Without democratic structures, the hierarchy finds it too easy to regard dissenting voices as nothing more than the imprudent cries of disgruntled and naive children, who do not really understand the needs of the Church. Democratic structures allow the will of the people to be communicated in a way that is necessarily heard, that is, through decision making processes that establish policies and laws. Democratic structures allow the equality of the people to be made manifest. The Church, therefore, needs to adopt a democratic form of government.

---

[31] Sidney E. Mead, *The Lively Experiment* (New York: Harper and Row, Publishers, 1963), pp. 82–83.

CHAPTER V

THE PERSONAL RIGHT TO RELIGIOUS FREEDOM

While admitting the validity of theological arguments in favor of democracy as a form of Church government, some would contend that democracy could never be realized within the Roman Catholic Church because the hierarchy would not grant the laity the freedom necessary to achieve democracy. The answer to this argument is found in the principle of religious freedom.

This argument not only minimizes the influence of the Spirit and of lay pressure on the hierarchy, but it also reveals a misunderstanding of both freedom and authority. It is an argument based upon the false assumption that the right to religious freedom is dispensed by the hierarchy. Such is not the case, however. The right to religious freedom is not bestowed; it inheres in the person and belongs to his nature. Thus, the dignity of the person is the foundation for the right to religious freedom, not the authority or the generosity of the hierarchy.

The basic question, then, is not whether the hierarchy will *grant* the freedom needed to democratize the Church. Rather, it is whether the individual will *exercise* his right to freedom against the pressures of those in authority who are more inclined to protect their lofty status than to render service in a spirit of equality and friendship. Present indications suggest that this right will be exercised with increasing vigor as the insights of the Declaration on Religious Freedom become more widespread. If there is an appropriate response from authority to the legitimate exercise of freedom, a peaceful democratization will occur. Structures will change to allow more people to participate in decision making processes. But if the response from authority is inappropriate, the result will be conflict. If authority becomes authoritarian, liberty will no doubt turn to license. It is important, therefore, if calamity is to be prevented, that the true nature of both freedom and authority be understood and that the priority of freedom be established.

Official documents of the Roman Catholic Church in the twentieth century have consistently proclaimed the dignity of the human person and affirmed the inviolable character of certain basic rights. Pope John XXIII in the encyclical *Mater et Magistra* reiterated and developed the social teachings of his predecessors. He cited Leo XIII's *Rerum Novarum* and Pius XI's *Quadragesimo Anno* as testimony to the fact that the Church asserts the basic dignity of the person and anchors her social teachings in that dignity.[1] In an article "On Religious Liberty," John Courtney Murray, S.J., says that the basic principles of the American constitutional system—inalienable rights and the protection of these rights by the government—"were clearly affirmed by Pius XII and by John XXIII."[2] The dignity of the human person was brought into sharp focus by John XXIII in *Pacem in Terris:*

> Any human society, if it is to be well-ordered and productive, must lay down as a foundation this principle: that every being is a person; his nature is endowed with intelligence and free will. By virtue of this, he has rights and duties of his own, flowing directly and simultaneously from his very nature, which are therefore universal, inviolable and inalienable. [n. 9][3]

The basic right is freedom. And this freedom concerns the whole of man's life—secular and religious. The social ency-

---

[1] *Seven Great Encyclicals* (Glen Rock, N.J.: Paulist Press, 1963), pp. 223, 225.
[2] In Culhane, *American Catholic Horizons*, p. 224.
[3] *Seven Great Encyclicals*, p. 291.

clicals of Leo XIII, Pius XI, Pius XII, John XXIII, and
Paul VI have clearly affirmed the right to freedom in secular
matters. Freedom in religious affairs was proclaimed un-
equivocally by the Second Vatican Council in the Declaration
on Religious Freedom: "This Vatican Synod declares that the
human person has a right to religious freedom" (n. 2).[4]
This statement, says Murray, in an introduction to the Declaration, can hardly be considered "a milestone in human history."[5] However, it is evidence of the fact that the Roman
Catholic Church is catching up with the times and supporting
the belief in religious freedom that is characteristic of many
pluralistic societies, particularly the United States.

A key section of the Declaration on Religious Freedom
reads as follows:

> This Vatican Synod declares that the human person has a right
> to religious freedom. This freedom means that all men are to be
> immune from coercion on the part of individuals or of social groups
> and of any human power, in such wise that in matters religious no
> one is to be forced to act in a manner contrary to his own beliefs.
> Nor is anyone to be restrained from acting in accordance with his
> own beliefs, whether privately or publicly, whether alone or in asso-
> ciation with others, within due limits.
>
> The Synod further declares that the right to religious freedom has
> its foundation in the very dignity of the human person, as this dig-
> nity is known through the revealed word of God and by reason itself.
> This right of the human person to religious freedom is to be recog-
> nized in the constitutional law whereby society is governed. Thus it
> is to become a civil right.
>
> It is in accordance with their dignity as persons—that is, beings
> endowed with reason and free will and therefore privileged to bear
> personal responsibility—that all men should be at once impelled by
> nature and also bound by a moral obligation to seek the truth, espe-
> cially religious truth. They are also bound to adhere to the truth,
> once it is known, and to order their whole lives in accord with the
> demands of truth.
>
> However, men cannot discharge these obligations in a manner in
> keeping with their own nature unless they enjoy immunity from ex-
> ternal coercion as well as psychological freedom. Therefore, the right
> to religious freedom has its foundation, not in the subjective disposi-
> tion of the person, but in his very nature. . . . [n. 2][6]

---

[4] Abbott, op. cit., p. 678.
[5] Ibid., p. 673.
[6] Ibid., pp. 678–679.

Certain parts of the above statement need to be singled out for special emphasis. Religious freedom means that "all men are to be immune from coercion on the part of individuals or of social groups or of any human power." A person is not "to be forced to act in a manner contrary to his own beliefs," nor is he "to be restrained from acting in accordance with his beliefs." Furthermore, free expression is not to be denied a person, "whether alone or in association with others." In the exercise of religious freedom, a person is to be free from *all* forms of coercion; he is entitled by nature even to "psychological freedom."

Now if such freedom belongs to a person in the world, it also belongs to a person in the Church. For there is no contradiction between nature and grace. They are mutually beneficial, compatible to the fullest measure, as can be seen in the person of Jesus, who according to Catholic belief is fully divine and fully human. Grace does not work against nature, but assists, improves, and perfects it. Grace builds on nature and qualifies it. "Being qualified," says Alois Muller, "means that the nature of a thing is not changed by grace, but that it is perfected and integrated into a higher order."[7]

The Declaration on Religious Freedom should have been more explicit about freedom *within* the Church. The Declaration should have presented freedom *within* the Church as the necessary concomitant of the personal right to religious freedom, thereby obviating some confusion. Nevertheless, the full implications of religious freedom will begin to emerge as the theological debate sparked by the Declaration begins to unfold.

Thus, in an introduction to the Declaration, Murray says: "The children of God, who receive this freedom as a gift from their Father through Christ in the Holy Spirit, assert it within the Church as well as within the world."[8] John L. McKenzie, S.J., takes a similar stand. He sees a connection between the failure of the Church to speak forthrightly on

---

[7] Muller, *Obedience in the Church*, p. 106.
[8] Abbott, *op. cit.*, p. 674.

religious freedom and its failure to allow its members to exercise the freedom that he regards as their inherent right as Christians. He says: "The Church can no more be convinced of the right of freedom of those who are not her members than she is convinced of the right of freedom of those who are her members."[9] But now that the Declaration shows that the hierarchy is convinced that the right to religious freedom is *universal,* it is to be expected that bishops will begin to encourage a greater exercise of freedom *within* the Church. For it would be absurd if the hierarchy continued proclaiming the universality of this right and at the same time continued to suppress the exercise of this right within the Church. Here the words written by Congregationalist John Wise in the early part of the eighteenth century are in order:

> And what! Is Man become so unfortunate, degraded and debased, as to be without all power in settling a Government over himself, relating to the matters of his Eternal Well-Being? Or when he comes back to a Fathers House, must he fall into the capacity of a meer passive Being and be put under such Rulers, as can easily turn Tyrants over him, and no relief for him in his own hands; this is certainly most repugnant to the Light of Nature and very disagreeable with the Liberty and free Genius of a Gospel State.[10]

The drive for freedom within the Roman Catholic Church —though largely uncoordinated—has begun. There is a deep stirring among the People of God, a restlessness, a growing impatience with the impacted residue of doctrinal and organizational excesses. In the Constitution on the Church the bishops speak of the laity's "right . . . to receive in abundance from their sacred pastors the spiritual goods of the Church"; they speak of the "just freedom which belongs to everyone in this earthly city" (n. 37).[11] Encouraged by these words, many Catholics are asking that these rights be spelled out in constitutional form and that the "just freedom" be made possible

---

[9] John L. McKenzie, S.J., "The Freedom of the Christian," *Religious Liberty: An End and a Beginning,* ed. John Courtney Murray, S.J. (New York: the Macmillan Company, 1966), pp. 104–105.
[10] John Wise, *A Vindication of the Government of the New-England Churches (1717),* introd. Perry Miller (Gainsville, Florida: Scholars' Facsimiles & Reprints, 1958), p. 66.
[11] Abbot, *op. cit.,* pp. 64–65.

in the form of new structures. The more freedom is discussed, the more it is desired. Daniel Callahan gives several examples of this: discussion about contraception escalates to speculation about a fallible magisterium; arguments about the religious liberty of other believers escalates to an affirmation of the "rights of the Catholic conscience"; conversation about renewal escalates to a demand for radical reform.[12]

The new emphasis on freedom has started a lively discussion on the nature of authority in the Church—is it absolute or limited? Alois Muller states: "With whatever difference of detail, most authors are agreed that today ecclesiastical authority must be limited by freedom."[13] Muller believes the time has come to eliminate the "relics of absolutism." By "absolutism" Muller means "the exercise of all power, legislative, juridical and executive, by one and the same authority, the subjects having at the most a right of appeal, but otherwise simply being 'governed.' "[14] To show that there is no scriptural basis for absolutism, Muller cites twenty-seven instances in the New Testament in which the exercise of authority is limited. Among the passages he quotes, the following are the most forceful:

[Matthew 20:25–28] But Jesus called them to him and said, "You know that the rulers of the Gentiles lord it over them, and their great men exercise authority over them. It shall not be so among you; but whoever would be great among you must be your slave; even as the Son of Man came not to be served but to serve, and to give his life as a ransom for many."

[Matthew 23:6–11] "They love . . . salutations in the Market places, and being called rabbi by men. But you are not to be called rabbi, for you have one teacher, and you are all brethren. And call no man your father on earth, for you have one Father, who is in heaven. Neither be called masters, for you have one master, the Christ. He who is greatest among you shall be your servant."

[Luke 22:25–27] And he said to them, "The kings of the Gentiles exercise lordship over them; and those in authority over them are

---

12 Daniel Callahan, "The New Freedom," *Commonweal*, LXXXII (June 18, 1965), 402.
13 Muller, *Obedience in the Church*, p. 169.
14 *Ibid.*, p. 148.

called benefactors. But not so with you; rather let the greatest among you become as the youngest, and the leader as one who serves. For which is the greater, one who sits at table, or one who serves? Is it not the one who sits at table? But I am among you as one who serves."

[John 13:12–15] "Do you know what I have done to you? You call call me Teacher and Lord; and you are right, for so I am. If I then, your Lord and Teacher, have washed your feet, you also ought to wash one another's feet. For I have given you an example, that you also should do as I have done to you."[15]

John L. McKenzie, S.J., says in his essay on "The Freedom of the Christian" that "Christian freedom and Christian equality go together. Any conception of inequality of persons destroys freedom. . . . Unless we are speaking of equality, we are not speaking of persons."[16] Because of the basic equality of all the faithful, the relationship between the laity and the servant hierarchy can and should be one of love. If, however, the relationship is one of obligation secured by the imposition of will rather than by love, authority is abused and the relationship is counterfeit. Says McKenzie: "There is an irremovable opposition between love and constraint."[17]

Arguing that authority is limited by a person's natural dignity, Donald Nicholl quotes from *Pacem in Terris:* "As authority is chiefly concerned with moral force, it follows that civil authority must appeal primarily to the conscience of individual citizens. . . . Since by nature all men are equal in human dignity, it follows that no one may be coerced to perform interior acts" (n. 48). Nicholl then makes the point that although Pope John is referring to civil authority, "what he has to say is just as applicable to ecclesiastical authority."[18]

The Constitution on the Church is quite clear about the role of those who exercise ecclesiastical authority: "Bishops govern the particular churches entrusted to them as the vicars and ambassadors of Christ . . . remembering that he who is

[15] *Ibid.,* pp. 24–29.
[16] In Murray, *Religious Liberty,* p. 98.
[17] McKenzie, *Authority in the Church,* p. 181.
[18] Donald Nicholl, "The Layman and Ecclesiastical Authority," *Clergy Review,* XLIX (July, 1964), 404.

greater should become as the lesser and he who is the more distinguished, as the servant" (n. 27).[19] The word "ambassador" in this passage is an appropriate selection. Ambassadors are representatives sent to kings and presidents. As such, they show a proper respect to the persons who receive them. Since the People of God are a kingdom of priests, members of the royal family of Christ, they are deserving of great respect, especially from the bishops, the ambassadors of Christ.

Another image used in the documents of Vatican II to designate the limitation of authority is "shepherd." Taken from scripture, this image is fitting not only because it suggests affection, but also because it implies that the true exercise of authority requires leadership, requires setting an example. In the Bible, says McKenzie, authority is synonymous with leadership. Paul is the pattern: "We have to postulate a rare personal relationship which enabled him to say to the Philippians naively, 'Do it the way I do it' (1:19–26 and 3:3–17)."[20]

A scriptural image that strongly recommends itself for contemplation to those in authority is that of Mary in relation to Christ. Apart from Christ, Mary is the paradigm of all authority in the Church. In building up the body of Christ, let bishops follow the method of Mary, who by example and kindness led her Son to mature freedom and responsibility. In the present age (of spiritual adolescence, perhaps) the children of God are more inclined to say to those over them that they are about their Father's business. Let the bishops not be angered about this. Rather, let them ponder what is being said. And if they think their authority is being challenged, let them speak tenderly, seeking compliance in humility rather than in indignation.

There are many images of scripture that reveal the way authority in the Church should be exercised. McKenzie cites the images of child, lackey, and slave as prime examples of

---

[19] Abbott, *op. cit.,* p. 51.
[20] McKenzie, *Authority in the Church,* p. 95.

the exercise of Church authority: "The greatest among the disciples should be a child (Mk 9:33–37; Mt 20:25–28; LK 9:46–48)"; the disciples should not copy the kings of the world and lord it over one another, but instead they should "be the lackey and slave of others (Mk 10:42–45; Mt 20:25–28; LK 22:24–30)."[21]

The call for the proper exercise of authority within the Church, though far from clarion, is growing louder. Edmund Hill, O.P., suggests that the Church should return to the pattern of freedom set by the early Christian community— "a Church (or rather Churches) organized as brotherhoods of free men, who were all endowed with an equal share in the messianic lordly authority of Christ himself."[22] Peter Riga speaks about a freedom in which "there can be no real subordination in ontological dignity. . . . Therefore, this episcopal function of authority cannot be a superiority or any type of domination."[23] The authority of the Church "must be a service freely accepted by men."[24] Daniel O'Hanlon, S.J., says that authority is to be conceived as a "compelling challenge to our free response" to the "love of God"; this is its "essential characteristic." The style of authority, continues O'Hanlon, is to be "simple and unostentatious," "exercised communally," "based upon open communication," "personal," "relaxed," and accompanied by "peace, joy, and good humor." Admittedly this kind of authority will be thought by many to be an "idealist madness." It therefore demands a "rare courage" if it is to be maintained.[25]

So far, not much of this "rare courage" has been in evidence since Vatican II. The exercise of authority is still

---

[21] John L. McKenzie, S.J., "Authority and Power in the New Testament," *Catholic Biblical Quarterly,* XXVI (October, 1966), 418.

[22] Edmund Hill, O.P., "Authority in the Church," *Clergy Review,* L August, 1965), 628.

[23] Peter Riga, *The Church Renewed* (New York: Sheed and Ward, 1966), p. 174.

[24] *Ibid.,* p. 175.

[25] Daniel J. O'Hanlon, S.J., "The Nature, Extent and Style of Authority in the Church," *Law for Liberty,* ed. James E. Biechler (Baltimore: Helicon Press, Inc., 1967), pp. 109–118.

reminiscent of an earlier age when absolutism was in vogue. Whereas other aspects of the Church have developed, authority seems resistant to the process of development. McKenzie says he would like to know why "authority in the Church, like liturgy, education, the press and communications, preaching and other activities of the Church, should not develop a theory and forms which are adapted to the twentieth-century man rather than to the sixteenth-century man." The point is, of course, that the present form of authority can change and will change. Says McKenzie: "Although the Church has yet to reflect the features of the democratic or republican state, there is no reason to think it will not."[26]

Now because freedom is a personal and inalienable right which takes precedence over and is served by authority, democracy seems preferable to monarchy as a form of Church government. The Church is supposed to be a community of free people, not a militaristic society in which command and rigidity are more important than love. Authority is supposed to serve the common good. But in practice authority tends to serve those who make the laws. If the rulers make the laws, authority tends to serve the rulers. Given the inclination of man to enslave himself, even a democracy can produce bad laws, but not any worse than those that a monarchy can produce. And if the freedom of the people is to be limited by bad laws, they themselves ought to bear the responsibility (and the guilt) for it, not their rulers.

Given the opposite tendency of man to fulfill himself, democracy again seems to work to the advantage of the people. For in a democracy laws that work against freedom can be changed, once the people are aware of what is happening. In a monarchy, however, even laws that are widely recognized as detrimental cannot be changed until the rulers (who may benefit from such laws) are willing to change them. And that may mean never. In comparison with monarchy, democracy offers a higher degree of freedom for a greater number of

---

26 McKenzie, *Authority in the Church*, p. 97.

people. Democracy is therefore a more desirable form of government for a Church interested in promoting the fulfillment (i.e., the holiness) of its members. For freedom is the desideratum for fulfillment. As the Council Fathers said in the Constitution on the Church in the Modern World, "only in freedom can man direct himself toward goodness."[27]

---

[27] Abbott, *op. cit.,* p. 214.

CHAPTER VI

THE EXPERIENTIAL BASIS
FOR ASSENT

Many bishops believe that monarchy is the form of government most suited, if not indispensable, to the needs of the Church. This could prove to be a sturdy obstacle in the road to a democratic Church. Still influenced by a formation more suited to the needs of an immigrant Church, these bishops might feel threatened by the many changes that lie ahead. Reacting to pressures put upon them, they might defend monarchy with a disproportionate enthusiasm, teaching that it is the form of government most suited to the needs of the Church. The laity would then feel bound in conscience to preserve monarchy. Thus, the process of democratization would be arrested. The answer to this argument may be found in the experiential basis for assent.

What one believes is conditioned by the totality of his experiences. Although a person is in principle free to believe, assent to a particular teaching in a concrete situation may not be possible. A variety of past experiences might weigh too heavily against assent. Consider, for example, a person who for ten years has eagerly pursued the goals of the John Birch Society. At the peak of his enthusiasm for the Society, he would be virtually incapable of assenting to the philosophy of, say, the Americans for Democratic Action. Only after a series of experiences altering his attitude toward the John Birch Society would he be inclined to join the ADA. Assent is triggered by a convergence of probabilities arising from a variety of personal experiences. On occasion, one very dramatic experience may produce assent, but this is quite rare. The hierarchy, therefore, cannot by mere proclamation force people to believe, especially if what they propose is contrary to the experience of the faithful. The fact that there is an experiential basis for assent provides an assurance that no insurmountable obstacle can be created by bishops teaching that monarchy is the best form of Church government.

It will be helpful at this point to distinguish between dogma and doctrine. Dogma refers to those propositions proclaimed by the pope as infallible and therefore as belonging to the indispensable core of Catholic belief, assent to which is necessary if a member is to be in good standing with the Church. Doctrine includes all dogma, but reaches out beyond dogma and encompasses many teachings that have never been proposed to the faithful as infallible. If non-dogmatic teachings are rejected by a believer, he may not be labeled a heretic or considered in poor standing with the Church.

Freedom and faith are inseparable. The Bishops of Vatican II say in the Declaration on Religious Freedom that "the act of faith is of its very nature a free act" (n. 9).[1] When a person becomes a Roman Catholic he assents to a core of dogmas. This act of faith is a free act. Should the Church define another dogma after a person enters the Church, he is confronted with a decision similar to the act of faith which brought him into the Church. Here again the act of faith is free. It is not proper to say without qualification that a person is obliged to believe a newly defined doctrine. In the words of Hans Küng: "A Christian has never to accept a dogma of the Church if it would be against his conscience."[2]

Granted that assent to dogma is free, is it not a different situation once a person has accepted all the dogmas of the Church? After all, if one accepts the dogma that the hierarchy

---

[1] Abbott, op. cit., p. 689.
[2] Hans Küng, Freedom Today, trans. Cecily Hastings (New York: Sheed and Ward, 1966), p. 56.

constitutes the official teaching authority of the Church, is he not obliged to follow the teachings of the hierarchy even in non-infallible matters? Whereas dogma includes the teaching that the hierarchy is the official teaching authority in the Church, dogma does not include the teaching that the hierarchy is always right, nor the teaching that a Catholic must accept every proposition the hierarchy advances. In *general*, a Catholic may be said to be obligated to assent to non-dogmatic teachings of the hierarchy. However, in the case of *particular* teachings, there may be any number of reasons why a person does not have such an obligation. He may have an expertise on a particular subject that renders his judgment more accurate than the collective judgment of the bishops. He may recoil at a teaching because it appears to him to be totally incompatible with common sense (which may be a sound guide when a person's outlook is more objective than that of the bishops). He may believe that he is under the inspiration of the Holy Spirit not to assent to a teaching that seems to be unauthentic.

Besides, it is somewhat irrelevant whether a person is obligated to believe a non-infallible teaching. Obligated or not, a person is apt to assent to a particular teaching in a concrete situation only when his past experiences are such that the teaching is acceptable to him. Alois Muller says that "in the matter of consent to a truth (teaching), the procedure does not lie in an act of the will but in that of a receptive mind." Further, "no consent is possible when there is a *contradiction between insight and teaching.*"[3] Apart from the enlightenment of grace (which builds on rather than obstructs human operations), belief is elicited by a convergence of probabilities. This is true relative to assent to basic dogmas (infallible teachings). It is also true relative to non-infallible teachings, especially those which advance the idea that monarchy is the form of

---

3 Alois Muller, "Authority and Obedience in the Church," *War, Poverty, Freedom: the Christian Response,* ed. Franz Bockle, Vol. XV of *Concilium,* ed. Edward H. Schillebeeckx, O.P., *et al* (New York: Paulist Press, 1966), p. 72.

government most compatible with the contemporary needs of the Roman Catholic Church.

To show that assent is not possible when there is a conflict between insight and teaching, it will be helpful to provide a philosophical explanation of why a person believes. For this we turn again to the seminal mind of John Henry Newman, who developed the concept of the *Illative Sense* in answering the question, "Why does a person believe?" In *An Essay in Aid of A Grammar of Assent* Newman establishes a basic grammar, or terminology, helpful in understanding the processes by which an act of faith is made. In an article entitled "Newman's 'Illative Sense,'" James O'Rourke, C.C., writes that the *Grammar of Assent* provides a "conclusive proof for religious enquiry on a philosophical basis."[4]

According to Newman, a person believes because of a convergence of probabilities. It is the force of accumulating probabilities that finally triggers assent. In the eighth chapter of the *Grammar of Assent* Newman describes the process by which the mind assents to a concrete proposition. In a concrete proposition *both terms point to something particular;* formal logic, however, requires that at least *one term of a proposition be abstract.* Describing how a person becomes certain of the concrete proposition that "Great Britain is an island," Newman argues that *formal logic* will not produce certitude in dealing with such a proposition. Assent to a concrete proposition is the result of a different kind of reasoning, namely, *ratiocination.* In opposition to formal logic, ratiocination is a kind of reasoning which is not subject to system. Ratiocination jumps from wholes to wholes, fastens on the concrete, and produces certitude in particular matters:

> It is plain that formal logical sequence is not in fact the method by which we are enabled to become certain of what is concrete; and it is equally plain, from what has already been suggested, what the real and necessary method is. It is the cumulation of probabilities, independent of each other, arising out of the nature and cir-

---

[4] James O'Rourke, C.C., "Newman's 'Illative Sense,'" *Irish Ecclesiastical Review,* LXT (March, 1963), 364–367.

cumstances of the particular case which is under review; proba-bilities too fine to avail separately, too subtle and circuitous to be convertible into syllogisms, too numerous and various for such con-version, even were they convertible. As a man's portrait differs from a sketch of him, in having, not merely a continuous outline, but all its details filled in, and shades and colors laid on and harmonized together, such is necessary for our reaching a concrete fact, com-pared with the rude operation of syllogistic treatment.[5]

Newman goes on to say that ratiocination is an act of the mind which reasons, "not from propositions to propositions, but from things to things, from concrete to concrete, from wholes to wholes."[6] This ratiocinative faculty, "in its perfection," is according to Newman the *Illative Sense*. Whereas logic is a system common to all minds, illation has no mold or system. The Illative Sense is unique in each person and follows principles of operation peculiar to the individual. "It is the mind that reasons, and that controls its own reasonings," says Newman, "not technical apparatus of words and propo-sitions."[7]

Explaining the unique operation of the Illative Sense, Newman says it seems in many cases to be a mark of genius. He gives as an example Sir Isaac Newton, who was able to perceive certain mathematical and physical truths even though proof was lacking. For a century and a half algebraists had used Newton's rule for determining imaginary equations without being able to prove mathematically that the rule was true. Some authors were ashamed to advance a proposition that depended on nothing but the insight of one man. Finally, the proof was discovered by a Professor Sylvester, much to everyone's relief. Other examples cited by Newman of the uniqueness of the operation of the Illative Sense are as fol-lows. Young boys are sometimes able to calculate with in-credible precision and great speed. They seem to have shortcuts which enable them to determine prime numbers up

---

[5] John Henry Newman, *An Essay in Aid of a Grammar of Assent*, introd. Etienne Gilson (Garden City, New York: Doubleday & Company, Inc., 1955), p. 230.
[6] *Ibid.*, p. 260.
[7] *Ibid.*, p. 276.

to seven places. Mature people also have this kind of genius. Napoleon, for example, was able to determine with uncanny accuracy from a brief observation the numerical force of 60,000 or 80,000 men, how long it would take them to come together if they were scattered, and how long it would be before they could attack.[8]

According to Newman, the Illative Sense is necessitated by the fact that man is a developing being subject to the law of progress. He assents to new particulars, new concrete propositions, not because of logic, but by a free movement of the mind that has its own way of arriving at certainty or truth. There is no need to devise, "what cannot be, some sufficient science of reasoning which may compel certitude in concrete conclusions." Such a science is impossible, says Newman. Logic is a science of reasoning which produces certitude in abstract conclusions, but there is no corresponding science of the concrete. Arriving at concrete conclusions is more of an art than a science. Newman says categorically that "there is no ultimate test of truth besides the testimony born to the truth by the mind itself." As confusing as this fact may be, says Newman, it is a "normal and inevitable characteristic of the mental constitution of a being like man on a stage such as the world. His progress is a living growth, not the formulas and contrivances of language."[9]

Logic produces a notional (or conditional) assent. Illation produces a real (or unconditional) assent. Logic involves what is common to many, illation what is unique to the individual. Logic depends upon abstraction, illation upon images derived from personal experience. Notional assent, says Newman, "is in itself an ordinary act of our common nature. All of us have the power of abstraction, and can be taught either to make or to enter into the same abstractions; and thus to cooperate in the establishment of a common measure between mind and mind." Real assent, however, prescinds from the abstract and therefore cannot be tested by a common norm. Says Newman:

[8] *Ibid.*, pp. 262–263.
[9] *Ibid.*, p. 275.

"We cannot make sure, for ourselves or others, of real apprehension and assent, because we have to secure first the images which are their objects, and these are often peculiar and special. They depend upon personal experience; and the experience of one man is not the experience of another. Real assent, then, as the experience which it presupposes, is proper to the individual."[10]

The image is of central importance in producing real assent. The more forceful the image, the more likely is the mind to assent. And after the initial act of assent, the stronger the image grows, the more likely is assent to endure. As far as assent is concerned, it is of little significance whether a given proposition is true or false. The significant thing is the prominence of the image. As Newman puts it: "A Proposition, be it ever so keenly apprehended, may be true or false. . . . An image, with the characters of perfect veracity and faithfulness, may be ever so distinct and eloquent an object presented before the mind . . . but, nevertheless, there may be no external reality in the case, corresponding to it, in spite of its impressiveness." A case in point for Newman is the belief held by certain men of science, namely, the belief that certain laws of nature are inviolable. "Philosophers of the school of Hume discard the very supposition of miracles, and scornfully refuse to hear evidence in their behalf in given instances, from their intimate experience of physical order and of the ever-recurring connexion of antecedent and consequent." In other words, the image of the inviolability of nature's laws has such attraction for the mind that it cannot consider another possibility. The question of truth or error is obliterated by the force of the image. The imagination has control and reason is dormant. Says Newman: "Their imagination usurps the functions of reason; and they cannot bring themselves even to entertain as a hypothesis (and this is all they are asked to do) a thought contrary to that vivid impression of which they are victims, that the uniformity of

---

[10] *Ibid.*, p. 82.

nature, which they witness hour by hour, is equivalent to a necessary, inviolable law."[11]

Just as the image is of central importance in producing assent, it is of equal importance in producing disbelief. A person changes his mind when the initial image which occasioned his assent weakens, grows to deformity, or becomes obscured by the presence of opposing images. The disintegration of assent is most likely to occur when a new set of probabilities cluster to form an image which eclipses the image formed by the initial synthesis of probabilities. Newman touches on this in *The Idea of a University,* in which he describes how a person falls into disbelief. He says that, although reason and revelation are harmonious, they may appear to be discordant. The appearance of inconsistency between reason and revelation may strike the imagination with such force that a man may fall into disbelief without reason coming into play at all. Let a man study the various secular disciplines, says Newman, and let him learn from "the astronomer that our sun is but one of a million central luminaries," from the geologist that "revolutions have been in progress through innumerable ages," from the comparative anatomist about "the minutely arranged system of organized nature," from the chemist and physicist about "the intricate laws to which nature, organic and inorganic, is subject," from the ethnologist about "the ramifications, and varieties, and fortunes of nations," from the antiquarian about "old cities laid bare, with the specific forms of human society once existing," from the linguist about the "slow formation and development of languages," from the psychologist, the physiologist, and the economist about the "subtle, complicated structure of the breathing, energetic, restless world of men." In short, "let him take and master the vastness of the view thus afforded him of nature, its infinite complexity, its awful colouring; and then, when he has for years drunk in and fed upon this vision, let him turn round to peruse the inspired records, or listen to the

---

[11] Ibid., pp. 80–81.

authoritative teaching of Revelation, the book of Genesis, or the warnings and prophecies of the Gospels." The shock might be so great that he would "experience a most distressing revulsion of feeling—not that his reason really deduces anything, but that his imagination is bewildered, and swims with the sense of ineffable distance of that faith from the view of things which is familiar to him, with its strangeness, and then again its rude simplicity, as he considers it, and its apparent poverty contrasted with the exuberant life and reality of his own world."[12] Assent, then, may disintegrate when the image upon which assent depends is no longer able to withstand the intrusion of opposing images. The greater the pressure from and vividness of opposing images, the greater the confusion and doubt. The breaking point comes, to repeat the words of Newman, when the "imagination is bewildered, and swims with the sense of ineffable distance of that faith from the . . . reality of one's own world."[13]

Let us now apply this process of entering into disbelief to the image of monarchy as the most desirable form of Church government. This image, of course, is a traditional one, still proposed by many members of the hierarchy and still held *notionally* by many of the faithful. If pressures for a democratic Church continue to increase, a majority of the bishops might develop an irrational attachment to monarchy, proposing it with even greater vigor for continued assent. In such a situation, what might logically be expected from the faithful? When a person is the product of a society governed by democratic practices, when he has been conditioned to motivate people in the context of democratic structures, when he has become convinced that democracy is more capable than monarchy of helping the greatest number of people achieve fulfillment, when he responds favorably to democratic processes and recoils instinctively to authoritarian decrees, when

---

[12] John Henry Newman, *The Idea of a University,* introd. George N. Shuster (Garden City, New York: Doubleday & Company, Inc., 1959), pp. 368–369.
[13] *Ibid.,* p. 369.

a great variety of past experiences coalesce to form a vivid and attractive image of democracy, he is not apt to embrace the proposition that monarchy is the best form of government to meet the contemporary needs of the Church. Rather, he is apt to be so repelled by the image of monarchy, once it is proposed to him for *real* assent, that he will be more convinced than ever of the need to democratize the Church. Imagine the absurdity of a situation in which bishops, having at the Council collectively proclaimed the principles which are, in effect, rationales for the democratization of the Church, return to their monarchical diocesan structures unaware of the significance of what they had proclaimed. Imagine the absurdity of a situation in which the bishops, having had several years of dialogue at the Council, return to their monarchical diocesan structures to become less responsive to the impulses of the Spirit than a large percentage of the laity. Imagine the absurdity of a situation in which bishops, having collectively extolled religious freedom as a personal and inalienable right, return to their dioceses and present to the faithful for their assent an image that connotes centuries of unfreedom, an image that suggests a type of authority inconsistent with the Gospel, an image that reeks of pride, power, and paternalism, namely, the image of monarchy. In such an absurd situation, the imagination would be bewildered. It would, in the words of Newman, swim "with the sense of ineffable distance of that faith . . . from the reality of one's own world." It would be incapable of assimilating the image of monarchy. Staggered by such a situation, some of the faithful would turn to invective against the hierarchy, some would leave the Church in disgust, and some would increase their efforts to democratize the Church.

It is, of course, highly improbable that a majority of bishops would be so affected by the oversights inherent in monarchical government that they would lose the insights of Vatican II. Though improbable, history testifies that such a thing is possible. One need only recall the Arian situation of the fourth century, when most of the bishops were heretical and most of the laity were faithful. Though unlikely, it is possible that the essentialist bishops, who were in the minority at the Council, could gain control of the content and language of official proclamations. This possibility must not be considered too remote, however, because essentialist bishops occupy many key positions in Church government and exert an influence proportionately greater than their numbers. But even if this possibility became a reality and official proclamations extolled monarchy over democracy, there would be little likelihood that the People of God would assent. If the image of democracy has grown to maturity in the minds of the People of God, official pronouncements at variance with this image would not produce assent. Such pronouncements might retard the democratization of the Church, but they would not curtail it. In fact, if the pronouncements were made too arrogantly or if they were buttressed by absurd reasoning, they would have an effect directly opposite of what was intended. Democratization would be accelerated.

A parallel situation, somewhat more advanced than the discussion on democracy, exists in the current debate on birth control. Just as the notion of monarchy seems incompatible with recent insights, so also does the notion that contraceptive birth control is wrong. New circumstances, such as population growth, biological discoveries, and psychological pressures have caused Catholics to adopt the practice of contraceptive birth control with increasing frequency. Official pronouncements opposed to contraception have had little effect on practice or belief. *Humanae Vitae,* which repeated traditional norms on birth control, met with widespread disbelief and vociferous opposition. A similar situation might prevail if official pronouncements were to deny the advantages of democracy as a form of Church government, now that the image of democracy has taken hold among the People of God. To illustrate by way of analogy, then, let us examine the question of birth control in greater detail.

In the matter of birth control there seems to be a growing reserve among the People of God toward the teaching authority of the Church. Not so long ago the writer listened to a couple make an embarrassing statement. They were the parents of twelve children. Whereas at one time they had regarded their large family as a sign of their fidelity to the Church, they had since come to regard it as a symbol of their gullibility. Echoing the thoughts of both parents, the husband said: "I used to feel proud about having a large family; and although I still love my children and wouldn't part with one of them, I now feel like a sucker." It is not likely that he will be quite so gullible in the future.

This "feeling like a sucker" might also be described as a "crisis of faith" or a "credibility gap." Whatever this incredulity is called, it is now more prevalent than before. Perhaps it is a natural reaction to what Gregory Baum calls "creeping infallibility." Because non-infallible teachings were frequently presented with the same firmness as were infallible teachings, Catholics tended to assent to both kinds of teaching in the same way. Although few Catholics would admit it, a good number of them acted as if the local bishop, the local pastor, and the sister teaching in the local school were all infallible. Specific examples of this "creeping infallibility" may still be found by polling the members of a Catholic congregation. In the fall of 1966, the writer asked a class of seventy-five adult Catholics the following question: "Does the Church teach *infallibly* that the use of contraceptives is intrinsically evil?" Two-thirds said yes. (This does not mean they believed or followed the teaching.) The people simply have not been trained to distinguish dogma from non-dogma.

The credibility gap has grown following the reports of the papal birth control commission, issued after two years of study by respected scholars and theologians of the Roman Catholic Church. Two reports were issued. The *majority* report, evolutionary in nature, argued for a change. The *minority* report, essentialist in nature, stood pat on the traditional formulas.

The majority report was drafted by the following: "the Rev. Joseph Fuchs, German Jesuit teaching at the Gregorian

University in Rome; the Rev. Raymond Sigmond, Hungarian Dominican, president of the Institute of Social Science of the Pontifical University of St. Thomas Aquinas; the Rev. Paul Anciaux, professor at the major seminary of Malines-Brussels, Belgium; the Rev. A. Auer, specialist in sexual questions, Wurzburg, Germany; the Rev. Michel Labourdette, O.P., theologian from Toulouse, France; and the Rev. Pierre de Locht of the National Family Pastoral Center, Brussels."[14]

The majority report says: "The morality of sexual acts between married people . . . does not then depend upon every particular act. Moreover the morality of every marital act depends upon the requirements of mutual love in all its aspects." The majority report then lists some of the reasons for this affirmation—developments in society, the new role of woman, lower infant mortality, a greater awareness of the importance of human sexuality, new discoveries in various fields of knowledge, and "the sense of the faithful." According to the sense of the faithful, "condemnation of a couple to a long and often heroic abstinence as the means to regulate conception, cannot be founded on truth." The majority report adds: "It is impossible to determine exhaustively by a general judgment and ahead of time for each individual case what these objective criteria will demand in the concrete situation of a couple." Placing the responsibility for the decision in such matters on the consciences of the individual couple, the majority report says: "Well instructed, and prudently educated as Christians, they will prudently and serenely decide what is truly for the good of the couple and of the children, and does not neglect their own personal Christian perfection, and is, therefore, what God revealing himself through the natural law and Christian revelation, sets before them to do."[15]

The minority report was drafted by the following: "Father John Ford, U. S. Jesuit on the faculty of the Catholic University, Washington; Father Jan Visser, Dutch Redemptorist who is rector of St. Alphonsus College, Rome; the Rev. Marceline

---

[14] *National Catholic Reporter*, April 19, 1967, p. 8.
[15] *Ibid.*

Zalba, Spanish Jesuit, a teacher of moral theology at the Gregorian University, Rome; and Father Stanley de Lestapis, S.J., sociologist and author, Vanves, France."[16]

The minority report says: "The Church cannot change her answer *because this answer is true.*" It would seem that a report on a topic of such gravity as birth control, drafted by eminent scholars, would not be so amateurish as to beg the question, which the above statement does. The very question which the commission was appointed to study was whether the traditional position was still valid, whether it was true.

Implicit in the minority report is a lack of awareness of the distinction between dogma and doctrine. While the Church cannot be wrong in the area of dogma, it can be wrong in the broader area of doctrine. The heart of the argument presented by the minority report is as follows: "The Church cannot substantially err in teaching doctrine which is most serious in its import for faith and morals, throughout all centuries or even one century, by imposing under serious obligation very grave burdens in the name of Jesus Christ, if Jesus Christ did not actually impose these burdens." Had the teaching on birth control been a matter of dogma, the minority argument might have been valid, but the teaching on birth control has never gone beyond the realm of mere doctrine. The simple truth is that in non-dogmatic matters the Church can be wrong. And if the question of birth control is finally decided in favor of the majority report, the following minority statement will be viewed not simply as false, but as an indictment of the Church, a confession of her obvious sins: "The Catholic Church could not have furnished in the name of Jesus Christ to so many of the faithful everywhere in the world, through so many centuries, the occasion for formal sin and spiritual ruin." It will be interesting to see how the essentialists explain away the admissions in the above statement if the majority statement becomes the official position of the Church. (One is

---

[16] *Ibid.*, p. 9.

reminded here of Robert McAfee Brown's remark that when the Church changes its position on birth control, the official pronouncement will begin with the following statement: "As the Church has always taught . . .") Quite frankly, the underlying reason for opposition to change in the matter of birth control seems to be less a matter of fidelity to traditional teaching than a matter of protecting the authority and prestige of those in power. Though stating it in a way that implies that it is the faithful and not the magisterium that is wrong, the minority position reveals that if a change in the teaching on birth control occurs, the faithful will no longer be so gullible and so easily led: "If the Church could err in such a way, the authority of the ordinary magisterium in moral matters would be thrown into question. The faithful could not put their trust in the magisterium's presentation of moral teaching, especially in sexual matters."[17]

On the one hand, then, the majority report says that the traditional teaching is wrong and should be changed. On the other hand, the minority report says that the teaching cannot change because the Church cannot change what it has previously taught. The London *Tablet* carried an editorial which succinctly expressed the papal predicament: "*Casti Connubii* was prompted by what in those days of 1930 was regarded as the moral laxity of the Lambeth Conference, which the Pope is now being invited to approve in preference to the teaching of his predecessor. It is obviously a far from easy invitation to accept."[18]

Following the publication of the reports of the papal birth control commission, Pope Paul uttered a non-definitive pronouncement that might at best be considered curious, at worst contradictory. He said he was delaying the long awaited decision because the conclusions of the commission could not be considered definitive. He went on to say that the traditional norms against artificial methods of birth control are still in force and that "it cannot be considered as if the teaching au-

---

[17] *Ibid.*, p. 10.
[18] "The Pope's Authority," *Tablet*, CCXX (June 11, 1966), 664.

thority (magisterium) of the Church were in a state of doubt."
No, the magisterium, he said, is simply "in a moment of study
and reflection." Some diocesan papers simply printed the
Pope's words or reaffirmed them editorially without commenting on the patent absurdity of the Pope's statement.
Robert Hoyt, however, editor of the lay controlled *National Catholic Reporter,* took the Pope to task for this
contradiction in an editorial entitled "Dubiously Doubtless":
"This is, surely, a puzzling combination of assertions. It
is difficult indeed to find a meaningful distinction between
a state of doubt and a 'moment of study and reflection.'
It is still more difficult to understand how anyone can say
he is not in a state of doubt and yet be unable to speak his
mind about it." Hoyt goes on to say that a statement is either
fallible or infallible. As long as the Pope is not speaking *ex
cathedra,* he can be in error. And the question of whether
the Church is now in doubt about birth control does not admit
of *ex cathedra* treatment. While the Pope deserves a hearing,
"the ordinary meaning of his words and the ordinary laws of
logic cannot be ignored in weighing his opinion. And we
do not envy the task of Msgr. Vallainc or any other spokesman
who must try to show that there is no doubt in the Church
about a teaching which has been the focal point of the most
intense theological debate in centuries."[19]

In the matter of birth control, the laity seem to be following
their own instincts. A *Newsweek* survey revealed that one
Catholic in three now uses contraceptives and that seven out
of ten want the Church to lift its ban.[20] When the evidence
from one's experience runs counter to official pronouncements
that seem not to be based on faith, and when a personal problem exerts considerable pressure, the simple result is that a
person makes up his own mind. If the voice of the "vicar
of Christ" does not seem to have a true ring to it, a person

---

[19] Robert Hoyt, "Dubiously Doubtless," *National Catholic Reporter,* November 9, 1966, p. 5.
[20] "How U.S. Catholics View Their Church," *Newsweek,* March 20, 1967,
p. 69.

has no choice but to follow the promptings of his own conscience, an authority Cardinal Newman once described as the "aboriginal vicar of Christ."[21] The acceptance or rejection of non-dogmatic teaching is determined primarily by one's personal experiences and insights, whether it is a matter of the form of birth control or the form of Church government. It is clear, says Muller, that "outside the sphere of infallibility, there remains no general rule for judging the truth of ecclesiastical pronouncements with certainty."[22] And therefore, if "enough considerations oppose themselves both to human faith and to human understanding or assent," Muller says elsewhere, "the intellectual answer to pronouncement will be doubt. Should these considerations be sufficiently weighty the official act may even have to be rejected altogether."[23] Clearly, the acceptance of hierarchical pronouncements depends upon the free assent of the People of God. Failure of the hierarchy to recognize this will undermine their own teaching authority.

Humanae Vitae is a case in point. According to John L. McKenzie, S.J., the encyclical greatly diminished the influence of papal authority, striking a blow from which the papacy might not recover for two or three hundred years, if at all. Opposition to the encyclical continues to mount. Even national hierarchies have felt compelled to qualify the document. According to *Time* magazine (October 4, 1968, p. 57), one national hierarchy after another "has modified, subtly or otherwise, the Pope's decree that 'each and every marriage act must remain open to the transmission of life.' " This modification is evident in the key statements, which the author of the *Time* article extracted from official pronouncements. Thus, the Dutch episcopate said: "Personal conscience cannot lightly pronounce itself on an encyclical of such authority, but personal conscience has the final word." The

---

[21] John Henry Newman, *Certain Difficulties Felt by Anglicans in Catholic Teaching,* 2 vols. (London: Longmans, Green, and Co., 1900), II, p. 248.
[22] Muller, *Obedience in the Church,* p. 272.
[23] *Ibid.,* p. 74.

bishops of West Germany allow deviation from papal norms for "serious reasons." The Belgian episcopate stated that a Catholic "who is capable of forming a well-founded judgment" on the issue of birth control "has the right to follow his conviction, provided that he remains sincerely disposed to continue his inquiry." The Austrian episcopate said that if Catholics reject the papal guidelines they "need not necessarily feel that they have separated themselves from God's love." The bishops of Britain asserted that "neither this encyclical nor any other document of the church takes away from us our right and duty to follow our conscience." The Canadian episcopate declared flatly that "whoever honestly chooses the course which seems right to him does so in good conscience." Had Pope Paul sufficiently applied the principle of collegiality, the encyclical would at least have enunciated the principle of free assent, which the bishops themselves subsequently asserted. As it is, the encyclical is for many of the faithful, and particularly for some theologians, both embarrassing and incredible.

While it is true that the non-dogmatic teaching of the Church demands that a person give "religious assent" to what is proposed for belief, it is not true that a person must surrender his common sense and accept a contradiction. In explaining the true meaning of religious assent, Gregory Baum says that "assent cannot be an unconditional surrender of the mind. This is impossible since teachings proposed as non-infallible are really fallible. There is no middle ground between fallible and infallible." Baum maintains that "the obedient response to authoritative teaching is, it seems to me, what the scholastics called *docilitas,* the readiness to learn." He then goes on to explain that the assimilation of teaching is not an easy process. The traditional teaching has been understood in a particular frame of reference. New teaching cannot simply be placed beside what was previously learned. It must be integrated into a vision of faith, absorbed into a total frame of reference. This, of course, requires an intense effort of the mind. Sometimes, says Baum, there will be situations in which a well-intentioned Catholic, obedient in all things, cannot accept a non-dogmatic teaching of the Church. After study and dialogue, he may still be unable to integrate this teaching into his vision of faith. It will lie barren in his mind, unproductive of life. Then, says Baum, "if the Catholic, obedient to the magisterium and open to dialogue, finds it impossible not only to assimilate a particular teaching but even to reconcile it at all with the total Gospel as preached by the Church, he may responsibly reveal his convictions and work toward a revision of the official position."[24] Now if this applies to teachings that are true, it applies even more strongly to teachings that may well be false, such as the teachings which favor rhythm over contraception and monarchy over democracy.

It is not to be expected that hierarchical statements which extol monarchy over democracy will automatically produce assent among the People of God. If the image of democracy is ripe in the minds of the People of God, arbitrary pronouncements against it by Church authorities will tend to produce disbelief. There is an experiential basis for assent and this is a necessary precondition for the acceptance of official pronouncements by Church authorities. According to Newman, a person believes because of a convergence of probabilities. The mere fact that in *general* a Catholic ought to assent to the teaching of the hierarchy does not necessitate his assent to a *particular* non-infallible teaching. When a particular teaching contradicts experience, there can be no authentic assent. Hume and his followers could not accept the belief in miracles because of their attachment to a particular image of the physical order; similarly, those whose experiences have forged in their minds a vivid and tenacious image of democracy would not be able to accept the teaching that monarchy is superior to democracy. The people schooled primarily in the images of the secular disciplines are easily confused and sometimes unbelieving when confronted by images that point to the mysteries

---

[24] Baum, "Teaching Authority of Vatican II," *loc. cit.*, pp. 92–93.

of religion; similarly, the People of God who have come to embrace a multiplicity of images that call forth an emotional response favorable to democracy will find themselves reeling in uncertainty and doubt when presented with the image of monarchy.

While it is true that the monarchical image has been dominant in the past, its vividness and attractive power lay primarily in the fact that it stood alone, unopposed by the image of democracy. Because monarchy was *the* form of government for the secular order, it was simply assumed that monarchy was the desideratum for Church government. The specific question as to the merits of democracy over monarchy in Church government was never raised as forcefully in the past as it has been in the last few years. In democratic countries the monarchical image has been eclipsed by the democratic image. Imaginatively, the People of God in democratic countries are now more attuned to democracy as a form of Church government even though conceptually and verbally many still cling to monarchy. It would seem that in the United States and in other democratic countries, democracy is becoming the object of *real* assent for Catholics. Monarchy may be the object of a fairly widespread *notional* assent, but even this is diminishing.

The difference between notional and real assent appears in the context of action. When a person has to act in a concrete situation, he acts in accordance with what he really believes, not in accordance with that to which he gives only notional assent. Confirmation of this statement is found in the practices of Catholics in the matter of birth control. Increasing numbers are repudiating the traditional teaching which proscribes contraceptives. Caught up in the pressures of modern life, many are impelled to re-examine the traditional teaching, to reject it, and to follow their own consciences. Seldom do they leave the Church now over the issue of birth control. Many simply reject the traditional teaching and go about their religious lives as usual. Official reiterations of the traditional position have little, if any, effect and sometimes lead to a challenging of the Church's teaching authority in other areas.

Now, what has happened in the area of birth control can be expected to happen in the area of Church government as well —official pronouncements will be treated casually. In a concrete situation, now that democracy has had an impact, the People of God are not apt to respond to authoritarian practices in great numbers. Catholics nowadays must be motivated democratically, if they are to be motivated adequately. Generally, they will not follow arbitrary commands to be involved in this or that activity. And unless they share in the decisions that terminate in this or that activity, they are not likely to be involved in an activity in more than a token way, even if exhortations to do so are made with great diplomacy. In general they will avoid involvement with the mission of the institutional Church. Should the hierarchy persist in the use of authoritarian and monarchical tactics, the People of God may recoil with antagonism. The ultimate result could be internal conflict and widespread disaffection.

The experiential basis for assent is not only the principle by which the difficulty arising from bishops teaching in favor of monarchy can be resolved. It is also a rationale for the democratization of the Church. Because faith is preconditioned by personal experience, the Church must present itself to the world in a frame of reference conducive to assent. If the Gospel is presented from a context of monarchy in a broader secular context of democracy, the possibility of assent is diminished. The image of monarchy tends to create a state of incredulity in the minds of many. Because of all that the image of monarchy suggests about the secular and religious governments of the past, people accustomed to democracy are apt to be suspicious of the motives that underlie statements by leaders in a monarchy, even when statements proclaim freedom. It is virtually impossible for an outsider looking in, if he is committed to democracy, to believe that the Church really believes in freedom when its monarchical structures seem to impede the exercise of freedom. If the Gospel message is to be believed by those who hear it, it must be lived by those who proclaim it. And if the Gospel message is pre-eminently about freedom, then the structures of the Church should manifest this freedom.

The Constitution on the Church in the Modern World says: "By virtue of her mission to shed on the whole world the radiance of the Gospel message . . . the Church stands forth as a sign of that brotherliness which allows honest dialogue and invigorates it." The mission of the Church requires that "we foster within the Church herself mutual esteem, reverence, and harmony, through the full recognition of lawful diversity. Thus all those who compose the one People of God, both pastors and the faithful in general, can engage in dialogue with ever abounding fruitfulness" (n. 92).[25] If there would be honest dialogue within the Church, those not in the Church might be more inclined to enter into dialogue with it. But under present structures there is little honest dialogue between clergy and laity. The Decree on Ecumenism says that in dialogue it is important that the opposite sides be able to "deal with each other on an equal footing."[26] Monarchical structures do not provide a common ground. They are not suited for dialogue. Instead, they tend to produce paternalistic utterances, the antithesis of dialogue. It would seem that democratic structures, in which people can come together on an equal footing, are necessary if the Church is to be "a sign of the brotherliness which allows honest dialogue and invigorates it."[27]

A precondition for dialogue is the belief that the other party is in good faith. As long as monarchical structures endure, sealing off internal dialogue, the Church will not appear to be truly interested in external dialogue. Statements encouraging dialogue will not ring true, and they will not be widely believed. As long as monarchy continues, dialogue will have many obstacles. Efforts to enter into dialogue will be viewed

---

[25] Abbott, *op. cit.*, pp. 305–306.
[26] *Ibid.*, p. 353.
[27] *Ibid.*, p. 306.

suspiciously and be easily interpreted as threats to freedom or as manipulations to achieve submission to Rome. However, if democracy takes hold in the Church and true internal dialogue develops, the credibility of the Church will increase. People not of the Roman Catholic Church will be more disposed to hear and to understand what it proclaims. Given the democratic experience of modern man, the possibility of assent to the Roman Catholic teaching would increase if this teaching emanated from a democratic structure. Clearly, the experiential basis of assent is a rationale for the democratization of the Church.

CHAPTER VII

THE SUPREMACY OF CONSCIENCE

The way many Catholics understand obedience creates another obstacle to the democratization of the Church. They believe that obedience to the hierarchy is always necessary. Hence, if bishops who feel a threat to their personal power and prestige would establish laws forbidding anyone to work toward the democratization of the Church, many, if not most, Catholics would be inclined to obey. Their consciences have not been trained to test hierarchical fiats, to distinguish between those laws promoting the comman good and those promoting the vested interests of the hierarchy. However, even though in general Catholics have not been taught explicitly to challenge or to disobey hierarchical commands when there are compelling reasons, such teaching is implicit in the principle of the supremacy of conscience.

In practice, the supremacy of conscience means the right to disobey. A person must follow his conscience even if it means disobeying the laws of the Church, even if it means excommunication. Excommunication does not cut a person off from God, nor does it prevent a person from pursuing his objectives, though it can create obstacles that prompt a person to resort to more dramatic measures. A person who follows his conscience cannot be stopped by a decree of excommunication. Without police power, the hierarchy has no way of preventing excommunicated persons from continuing their educational and organizational efforts toward a democratic Church.

The laws of the Church are secondary to the law of the Spirit. The law of the Spirit is one which frees. Church laws are enacted to assist the law of the Spirit. When the law of the Spirit conflicts with a law of the Church, the law of the Spirit is to be followed. Bernard Haring says that the law of the Spirit means "that God expresses his holy will by his gifts. And we accept in gratitude, in the spirit of childhood, the very gifts of God as the rule of our life."[1] Now if a person believes democracy to be a gift of God for the Church, he may in good conscience work toward a democratic Church, even though Church laws might forbid such action. William P. Lynch, S.J., writes as follows: "Therefore, Paul can say to the Christian: You are no longer under the law, but under grace (Rom. 6:14). . . . St. Thomas tells us that the new Law is the Law of the Spirit, that this law is actually identical with the person and the activity of the Holy Spirit dwelling in us. 'It is the Holy Spirit himself . . . producing in us love, the plentitude of the Law.' "[2]

Because the law of the Spirit is coming into greater prominence, more voices are registering complaints about the rigidity of canon law and the widespread misuse of authority. Peter Huising, S.J., says that "a completely new law is required, bearing on the contemporary condition of the Church's life and expressed in contemporary language."[3] Cardinal Leger declares: "It is one of the main duties of authority to initiate and to cooperate with initiative, not to allow itself to become merely the final rank in a juridical setup."[4]

---

[1] Bernard Haring, C.Ss.R., "The Law Must Free," *Ave Maria*, XCVIII (September 7, 1963), 16.
[2] William P. Lynch, S.J., "The Problem of Freedom," *Cross Currents*, X (Spring, 1960), 114.
[3] Peter Huising, S.J., "The Reform of Canon Law," *Religious Freedom*, ed. Neophytos Edelby and Teodoro Jiminez-Urresti, Vol. XVIII of *Concilium*, ed. Edward H. Schillebeeckx, O.P., *et al.* (New York: Paulist Press, 1965), p. 121.
[4] Paul Emile Leger, "The Church and Mankind," *Jubilee*, XIII (September, 1965), 17.

Though much discussion today concerns the system of ruling authority in general, a good portion focuses on the papacy itself. For the pope is regarded by Catholics as the supreme governing power in the Church. It is clear from what many Catholic thinkers are saying, however, that "supreme" does not mean "absolute." Papal power, though supreme, is limited, at least in principle. In practice, though, absolutistic tendencies creep in. Following the First Vatican Council, which asserted the primacy of the pope, a group of papalists went beyond the intent of the Council, making exaggerated claims for papal authority. Such claims were possible because the Council had asserted the primacy of the pope without defining the limits of his authority. The tendency of the papalists to ascribe absolute powers to the pope triggered a response from the German hierarchy which established quite clearly that papal authority is not absolute. The response was the Declaration of the German Hierarchy. This declaration, issued in 1875, came to be regarded as the official Vatican position on papal primacy. It was not only accepted by the English bishops and by Cardinal Dechamp of Malines, but even by Pius IX. According to Pius IX, the declaration "is an expression of that true Catholic doctrine which is at once the teaching of the Vatican Council and of the Holy See." The declaration *rejected* the following propositions:

(1) Through the Vatican decisions, the Pope has reached the position of taking the rights of the bishops in every single diocese into his own hands and substituting the papal authority for that of national episcopate.

(2) Episcopal jurisdiction has been absorbed into papal.

(3) The Pope no longer, as hitherto, exercises certain reserved rights, but holds the whole of the bishops' rights in his hands.

(4) He has in principle taken the place of each individual bishop.

(5) It rests entirely with the Pope whether he will, in practice, at any given moment, take the place of the bishop in relation to governments.

(6) The bishops are now no more than his tools, his officials, without responsibility of their own.

(7) In relation to Governments, they become the officials of a foreign sovereign, and furthermore, of a sovereign whose infallibility

makes him totally absolute, beyond any absolute monarch in the world.[5]

According to Küng, it is also evident from an examination of texts of the discussions at the First Vatican Council that the authority of the pope is "not absolute" and "not arbitrary."[6] Küng maintains that papal primacy is limited not only by natural law, which forbids absolutism and arbitrariness, but also by many things in the Church, including the following: "the existence of the episcopate"; "the orderly exercise of office by the bishops"; "the aim of the pope's direction of office: . . . the service character"; "the mode and manner of papal direction of office."[7]

Although some parts of canon law seem to give the pope absolute power, other parts show that his power is limited. Canon 1556 "clearly states," says Küng, "the first see is under judgment of nobody. Accordingly, no earthly, no state, and no ecclesiastical power or institution is recognized as competent to stand in judgment over the papacy." But, according to Küng, "it cannot be denied that a very wide chasm yawns between papal claims and historical fact." The evidence of history does not support the theory set forth by Canon 1556. The plain fact is that popes were frequently deposed. Küng does not base his historical argument on the Arian tribunals of the fourth century (in which powers alien to the Church effected papal depositions), but on the depositions that occurred in the Middle Ages. Citing H. Zimmermann, Maassen, L. Duchesne, E. Caspar, A. Fliche and V. Martin, J. Haller and F. X. Seppert, Küng argues that the document *Prima sedes,* upon which Canon 1556 is based, "clearly goes back to a sixth century forgery."[8] Furthermore, the historical facts are that a whole series of papal trials occurred from the earliest

5 Hans Küng, *The Council in Action* (New York: Sheed and Ward, 1963), pp. 231–232.
6 Hans Küng, *Structures of the Church,* trans. Salvatore Attanasio (New York: Thomas Nelson & Sons, 1964), p. 233.
7 *Ibid.,* pp. 234–236.
8 *Ibid.,* p. 251.

times down to the fifteenth century. "The participants in the papal elections, the clergy and the people of Rome, as well as the emperor, also pronounced the sentences deposing the pontiffs."[9]

The proper interpretation of canon law reveals quite clearly that papal authority is not absolute. Küng cites the the classic manual on canon law by F. X. Wernz, "the famous Roman canonist, consultor of the Roman congregation, . . . rector of the papal Gregorian University . . . Jesuit General (1906 to 1914)." The manual shows that according to canon law the pope can lose his authority or office in five instances: death, resignation, mental illness, heresy, schism. Thus the manual reads: "Upon death the spiritual and civil power of the Roman Pontiff ceases. . . . Upon resignation. . . . Also through mental illness. . . . By heresy notoriously and openly manifested. . . . Schism is rightly considered to be on the same level as heresy. . . ."[10] (Schism would mean that the pope would separate himself from the rest of the Church or that he would not share communion or the sacraments.) Küng goes on to explain that when a council deposes a pope they do not actually remove him from office, but declare that he has removed himself from office by his deeds. He uses the issuance of a death certificate as an analogy. The death certificate simply declares what has occurred; it does not cause the death. Similarly, a conciliar statement merely certifies the separation of a person from the the office of the papacy.[11]

According to Küng, the fifteenth century Council of Constance demonstrates conclusively that a council has the power to depose a pope. There were three men claiming the office of the papacy, all of whom were deposed by the Council of Constance against their will. A trial against John XXIII led to his removal from office (May 9, 1415). The two other claimants to the papal office were expected to resign. Gregory

---

[9] *Ibid.*, p. 252.
[10] *Ibid.*, pp. 257–258.
[11] *Ibid.*, p. 257.

refused, even after he was formally granted the right of con-
vocation of the Council (April 7, 1417). Benedict XII was officially deposed (July 26, 1417). Ultimately, Martin V was
elected pope.[12] As Küng sees it, the "legitimacy of Martin V
and all other subsequent popes up to the present day depends
on the legitimacy of the Council of Constance and its procedure in the question of the popes."[13]

It appears from what Küng has said that in practice as well
as in theory the governing power of the pope is limited. And
if the "supreme" governing power is limited, so also is the
governing power of the hierarchy. Now, if the hierarchy may
assert themselves against the pope when they are convinced
conditions allow it, it is also true that the laity may assert
themselves against the pope (and the hierarchy) when they
are convinced that conditions allow it. The basic right that
sanctions a disobedient act is the right to follow one's conscience.

The remarks about conscience by John Henry Newman are
helpful in showing that even the governing power of the pope
is limited by conscience. Newman understands conscience as
a judgment that is made when a specific act is contemplated
here and now. He adopts the definition given by Aquinas as
his own: "I observe that conscience is not a judgment upon
any speculative truth, any abstract doctrine, but bears imme-
diately on conduct, on something to be done or not done.
'Conscience,' says St. Thomas, 'is the practical judgment or
dictate of reason, by which we judge what *hic et nunc* is to
be done as being good, or to be avoided as evil.' "[14] According
to Newman, conscience does not conflict with infallibility, but
with command or law: "Conscience being a practical dictate,
a collision is possible between it and the Pope's authority only
when the Pope legislates, or gives particular orders, and the
like. But a Pope is not infallible in his laws, nor his com-

---

12 *Ibid.*, pp. 269–270.
13 *Ibid.*, p. 270.
14 Newman, *A Letter Addressed to His Grace the Duke of Norfolk*, p. 69.

mands, nor in his acts of state, nor in his administration, nor in his public policy."[15] Newman cites a hypothetical example to show that papal command is limited by conscience. If, for example, says Newman, the pope commanded the English bishops to order their priests to work toward the establishment of teetotalism and one of the priests was fully convinced this would be wrong but followed the command anyway, he would "commit a sin *hic et nunc* if he obeyed the Pope, whether he was right or wrong in his opinion, and if wrong, although he had not taken proper pains to get at the truth of the matter."[16] Newman concludes his discussion on conscience with a remark that has been quoted many times, not only for its levity, but also for its truth: "Certainly, if I am obliged to bring religion into afterdinner toasts, (which indeed does not seem quite the thing), I shall drink—to the Pope, if you please—still, to Conscience first, and to the Pope afterwards."[17]

Contemporary theologians echo the thoughts of Newman. Muller quotes A. deBovis, who says categorically: "The power of the magisterium alone . . . possesses the privilege of infallibility; the power of jurisdiction or the canonical power does not have it."[18] Karl Rahner says that "the subject has the duty in conscience of examining the moral admissibility of what has been commanded."[19] Bernard Haring writes: "An inculpably erroneous dictate of conscience obliges the same as a correct conscience, just as a servant feels obliged to carry out the order of his master as he has understood it if he listened attentively even though the command was actually different."[20] In the words of Hans Küng: "It is universally held in Catholic moral theology that conscience is the immediate norm of conduct in every case. Thus there is a true primacy of the

15 *Ibid.*
16 *Ibid.*, p. 64.
17 *Ibid.* p. 66.
18 Muller, *Obedience in the Church*, p. 69.
19 Karl Rahner, S.J., *The Christian in the Market Place*, trans. Cecily Hastings (New York: Sheed and Ward, 1966), p. 178.
20 Bernard Haring, C.Ss.R., *The Law of Christ*, Vol. I: *General Moral Theology*, trans. Edwin G. Kaiser (Westminster, Maryland: Newman Press, 1961), p. 154.

subjective conscience over every objective norm."[21] Bishop Wright says: "Authority depends on conscience not only for the holy exercise of its claims; it depends on conscience for the very acceptance of these. The authority, that of the Pope included, which would be unmindful of conscience or hold it in contempt would be suicidal, destructive of itself."[22] Muller writes that "according to Archbishop Roberts, 'it is humanly impossible to exercise authority without consulting the governed. To deny this is to make nonsense of obedience.' "[23] Schillebeeckx says that the laity may revolt if their rights are not spelled out. The rights of the priests, he says, are set forth in canon law. Therefore, the layman also "should be given canonical *protection.*" Otherwise, "after enduring as many conflicts as he can support," he may "throw over the whole enterprise."[24] Commenting on the relationship between authority and obedience, McKenzie states: "When authority habitually fails to command the right thing, it no longer serves the end of society, and it cannot command the obedience."[25] Again, "authority itself may act in opposition to the end of society, and then disobedience becomes not only a right but a duty."[26] In a chapter on leadership, McKenzie says: "In a given situation, command may not only be an inept means toward the end, it may positively interdict the attainment of the end. When this happens, the only moral response to a command is disobedience."[27]

In the past it often happened that a person in conflict with authority would leave the Church. But there is another option, and that is to stay and fight, to enter into open conflict with those who misuse authority. Increasingly, Catholics are taking the latter course of action. Hopefully, the growing conflict

---

[21] Küng, *The Council in Action*, p. 202.
[22] John J. Wright, "Reflections on Conscience and Authority," *Critic*, XXII (April-May, 1964), 25.
[23] Muller, *Obedience in the Church*, p. 152.
[24] Edward H. Schillebeeckx, O.P., "The Layman in the Church," *Thomist*, XXVII (April, 1963), 282.
[25] McKenzie, *Authority in the Church*, p. 11.
[26] *Ibid.*, p. 7.
[27] *Ibid.*, p. 90.

between the rights of authority and the rights of conscience will result in the embracing of truth, either by those in authority if their commands are proven inappropriate, or by those under authority if their consciences are proven to be incorrectly formed.

The faithful who are convinced in conscience that democracy is the best form of Church government are not bound to follow commands against activity leading to a democratic Church. Even if they are excommunicated for their disobedience, they can still pursue their goals, as the hierarchy does not have police power. Excommunicated Catholics may be kept out of Churches, but they can still meet, organize, speak publicly, and use the mass communications media to further their objectives. If the excommunicated Catholics have a valid message and present it well, unexcommunicated Catholics, including some bishops, can be expected to take up the fight. As the pressure for democracy becomes more intense, the bishops opposing democracy would be forced to spend more of their time confronting the issue. They would be compelled to wrestle with the arguments of their opponents in an attempt to justify their opposition to democracy. Similarly, those supporting the democratic idea would have to come to grips with the arguments set forth against it. Ultimately, truth could be expected to emerge. Bishops opposed to democracy who issued commands in good conscience should be able to accept democracy once it is seen to be of the Spirit. Whatever the outcome, conscience must be followed. The person in authority must follow his conscience in issuing commands, and not be unduly influenced by those who disobey. The person under authority must follow his conscience in responding to commands, even if it means disobedience and excommunication. If either side yields prematurely, the evolution of the issue may be delayed.

It is clear, therefore, that because conscience is supreme in particular situations, democracy may be pursued in spite of laws to the contrary. And because democratic processes provide a matrix more conducive to the training and refinement of conscience, the principle of the supremacy of conscience provides, in effect, a rationale for the democratization of the Church. A person whose conscience is properly trained decides a specific issue for himself, after taking into account all relevant factors. A person whose conscience is not properly trained lets someone else make his decisions for him.

Because of monarchical structures, the consciences of many Catholics have been dulled. They have frequently relied too heavily on the consciences of those who formed the laws. Generally, they have not been trained to question whether a specific law is good or bad. Since in a democracy the people share in the processes that establish laws, there is a greater sophistication about law than in a monarchy. In a monarchy the people have no direct means (apart from revolution) of changing the laws or removing their leaders. Consequently, they spend little or no time thinking about the merits of one potential leader versus another or of one type of law versus another.

It seems regrettable that in a democracy, where protest is acceptable (to a degree), that the Church, commissioned as it is to prick consciences, tends (because of monarchical structures) to deaden consciences. The violence of modern times (Nazi Germany, ghetto poverty, Vietnam, and the threat of nuclear destruction) demands that people be trained to make their own decisions. Too much is at stake to pass the responsibilities on to others. The People of God must be trained to decide responsibly in freedom. Democracy is much more conducive to this end than monarchy.

CHAPTER VIII

THE PRINCIPLE OF SUBSIDIARITY

The principle of subsidiarity answers the objection that a democratic Church would weaken authority and diminish the power of the Church to achieve its purposes. In support of the notion that democracy weakens authority in the Church, one might be inclined to cite the tradition of the Free Churches. The Baptists, for example, have been quite vocal in support of democracy in the Church. Yet the Baptist leaders have little authority, according to Paul Harrison, who is himself a Baptist. Harrison says that Baptist leaders lack authority, not because they have democracy, but because they *lack* democracy. "For years," says Harrison, "the Baptists have been looking at anarchy and seeing democracy."[1] This is not to say that Baptist leaders have no power. They do. But often the power is not adequately distributed, and it is not always responsible to the people at the grass roots level. Consequently, the determinations of power "are as likely to be derived from culture as from Christ."[2]

Harrison points out that in many denominations the officers are constantly struggling against the danger of institutional

---

[1] Paul M. Harrison, *Authority and Power in the Free Church Tradition* (New Jersey: Princeton University Press, 1958), p. 158.
[2] *Ibid.*

chaos. He says that in order to "preserve pure democracy" the Baptists have built into their system of government many contradictions. "To absolutize in principle the idea of local autonomy and to create, at the same time, associational organizations which compromise the absolute, is a contradiction. It is often observed that the Baptists are preoccupied with checks and balances. This is inaccurate. Actually, they have been primarily interested in checks." Because of this lack of balance, the Baptists have recruited people for executive positions who have a high degree of personal charisma. Able to accomplish organizational objectives by virtue of their personal magnetism, expertise, and genius, they are able also to accomplish personal objectives—staying in power and increasing control. Once securely situated in a position of power, a Baptist executive officer is not apt to be removed. Ultimately, his control is so pronounced that the association he heads is more apt to respond to his power than to give him direction. Says Harrison: "The fundamental anomaly in the Baptist situation . . . is that despite their noblest effort, the Baptists have not succeeded in their program to check authority and to balance power."[3]

Comparing the associational executives with Roman Catholic hierarchical executives, Harrison says: "The Baptists may have been wise when they removed the bishops from their places, but when they also eliminated the ecclesiastical authority of their own associations, the bishops returned in business suits to direct affairs from behind the curtain of the center stage." In other words, the Baptists never fully succeeded in their attempt to control Church leaders. In fact, the present situation may give certain Baptist officers power over the people that exceeds even that of bishops. "Since their responsibilities are prodigious, their power is unrestricted because their authority is so limited." According to Harrison, authority is not simply a grant to power, "it also defines and limits power." Hence, if Baptists want leaders who exercise

---

[3] *Ibid.,* p. 78.

a representative rather than arbitrary power, they must grant real authority, not merely responsibility, to their leaders, so that authority can be revoked when power is used arbitrarily.[4]

Catholics, on the other hand, must decentralize the power of their Church. Power must be shared, if the purposes of the Church are to be achieved, that is, if the Word of God is to be proclaimed faithfully and if the world is to be served effectively. Catholics may have felt it necessary during times of stress to allow their leaders to exercise almost unlimited power. But in surrendering their power to their leaders, Catholics surrendered much of their effectiveness in witnessing to the Word and in serving the world. Power being centralized, many bishops fail to see the importance of developing lay leaders capable of independent action. Accustomed to motivating by decree, many bishops are hamstrung in situations demanding a knowledge of group dynamics and psychological motivation. Consequently, many outstanding laymen avoid Church organizations and seek other avenues of fulfillment. The bishops are left with lackeys who wait for orders from above and who say yes to almost any command, no matter how unsuited it is for achieving the purposes of the Church. As a result, the power of the institutional Church is neutralized. To be effective, the Church must decentralize.

To decentralize is not to weaken authority. As a matter of fact, democracy strengthens authority. According to William H. DuBay, "nowhere is civil authority more respected than in a democracy." DuBay gives a number of reasons for this. For one thing, the function of authority in relation to the people is more clearly defined. Leaders are not invested with the mythical notion that they have prerogatives beyond those of the society they govern. For another thing, the processes of democracy lessen the possibility of corruption and irresponsibility. Whereas the monarch was once regarded as having a divine right to privacy, the public official in a democracy must give an accounting to the people for all of his words

---

[4] *Ibid.*, p. 227.

and deeds that touch upon his public responsibility. The reason for this is that official action should be exposed to public scrutiny and criticism. For still another thing, the processes of democracy help to keep the officials better informed about the conditions and needs of society. The leaders, if they are to remain in office, need to know the feelings and ideas of their constituents. Says DuBay: "Familiarity with the factual situation is the *sine qua non* of effective government."[5] If democracy strengthens secular authority, it will strengthen religious authority as well.

Perhaps the basic reason why democracy strengthens authority can be found in the principle of subsidiarity. This principle has long been a part of the Church's social teaching. It had its roots in Leo XIII's *Rerum Novarum,* which proclaimed the workers' right to organize, and flowered in the beauty of *Quadragesimo Anno,* issued by Pope Pius XI in 1931. In substance, here is the principle of subsidiarity:

79. It is indeed true, as history clearly shows, that owing to the change in social conditions, much that was formerly done by small bodies can nowadays be accomplished only by large organizations. Nevertheless, it is a fundamental principle of social philosophy, fixed and unchangeable, that one should not withdraw from individuals and commit to the community what they can accomplish by their own enterprise and industry. So, too, it is an injustice, and at the same time a grave evil and a disturbance of right order, to transfer to the larger and higher collectivity functions which can be performed and provided for by lesser and subordinate bodies. Inasmuch as every social activity should, by its very nature, prove a help to members of the body social, it should never destroy or absorb them.

80. The State authorities should leave to other bodies the care and expediting of business and activities of lesser moment, which otherwise become for it a source of great distraction. It then will perform with greater freedom, vigor, and effectiveness, the tasks belonging properly to it, and which it alone can accomplish, directing, supervising, encouraging, restraining, as circumstances suggest or necessity demands. Let those in power, therefore, be convinced that the more faithfully the principle of "subsidiarity" is followed and a hierarchical order prevails among the various organizations, the more excellent will be the authority and efficiency of society, and

---

[5] DuBay, *The Human Church,* p. 152.

the happier and more prosperous the condition of the common-wealth.[6]

The principle of subsidiarity applies to the Church as well as to the State. It applies, says Pius XII, "to every order of social life, even to the life of the Church, without prejudice to her hierarchical structure."[7] Writing on "Government in Religious Life," Ladislas Orsy says frankly: "There is no good government without an honest respect for the so-called principle of subsidiarity. This principle enunciates a law valid for any society or community."[8] In an article on "The Use of Authority" John Meany says that the principle of subsidiarity is a "principle whose reasonableness is self-evident."[9]

The principle of subsidiarity must be applied within the Church if pastoral goals are to be met. "Go into the whole world" is a commission to enter into dialogue. To be social means to be able to converse. But dialogue cannot occur unless there are structures for dialogue, situations in which people can come together for pertinent discussion. The Church must undergo a process of "socialization," a word Pope John uses in *Mater et Magistra* to describe the conditioning process which enables a man to become more human by entering into a greater number of relationships. In *The Other Dialogue* Joseph Gremillion, secretary of the papal commission on world justice and peace, explains that socialization means the "multiplication of social relationships."[10] As Gremillion sees things, it is imperative that the Church increase the number of its subsidiary structures, so that additional relationships can be established for dialogue. Now, more than ever, the principle of subsidiarity must be applied within the Church.

---

[6] Pius XI, "Quadragesimo Anno," *Seven Great Encyclicals* (Glen Rock, N.J.: Paulist Press, 1963), pp. 147–148.

[7] Pius XII, "Allocution of February 2, 1946," quoted in Hans Küng, *The Council in Action* (New York: Sheed and Ward, 1963), p. 252.

[8] Ladislas Orsy, "Government in Religious Life," Supplement in *The Way*, II (May, 1966), 105.

[9] John Meany, "The Use of Authority," *America*, CXIV (March 26, 1966), 408.

[10] Joseph Gremillion, *The Other Dialogue* (New York: Doubleday & Company, Inc., 1965), p. 47.

Because the principle of subsidiarity has gained widespread acceptance, and because traditional structures are feeling the strain of modern life, Catholic thinkers are urging major changes in the way the Church is governed. James A. Coriden, past president of the Canon Law Society, says that the change in organizational and structural forms parallels the development of dogma. The Church passes from one age to another and reacts to a variety of cultural conditions; changes of structure and procedure are incorporated. The changes that are wrought are not simply the accidents of historical encounter; they are indispensable to the growth of the Church. Says Coriden: the pattern of adaptation and change "appears to be a mandate based on the very nature of the Church, just as growth and development are inherent in the nature of a living organism." This fact is of central importance, for "it is the motive for the whole effort toward renewal and relevancy. It sums up the basis for a fearless adaptation of forms and structures."[11]

We need, says Rock Caporale, S.J., a "mechanism of ongoing self-analysis"; he argues for the "institutionalization of change itself."[12] "We are," says John Courtney Murray, S.J., "on the eve of some important structural changes."[13] Ecumenist Daniel O'Hanlon, S.J., proposes that Catholics emulate the Free Churches in their "willingness to accept new forms."[14] Gregory Baum, O.S.A., proposes "more independence for episcopal conferences, with legislative power to apply and adapt the general norms valid for the Church Universal."[15]

---

[11] Letter by James A. Coriden, quoted in Bernard Lonergan, S.J., "The Transition from a Classicist World-View to Historical Mindedness," *Law for Liberty*, ed. James E. Biechler (Baltimore: Helicon Press, Inc., 1967), p. 126.

[12] Rock Caporale, S.J., *Vatican II: Last of the Councils* (Baltimore: Helicon, 1964), pp. 179–180.

[13] Murray, *Religious Liberty*, p. 106.

[14] Daniel O'Hanlon, S.J., "What Can Catholics Learn from the Free Churches?," *Do We Know the Others?*, ed. Hans Küng, Vol. XIV of *Concilium*, ed. Edward H. Schillebeeckx, O.P., *et al.* (New York: Paulist Press, 1966), p. 112.

[15] Gregory Baum, O.S.A., "Away from Centralization," *Clergy Review*, XLVIII (May, 1963), 277.

Hans Küng hopes that the international synod of bishops will meet certain basic requirements: that it will "convene periodically," that bishops will be elected for "fixed periods of time," that they will have "legislative power," and that they will represent "all nations and continents."[16] Joseph O'Donohue proposes a popular election of bishops, including a ten-year term for the pope. He thinks that election of officers will result in an "emphasis on the 'collective nature of shared responsibility,' " a "rotation in office of appointive aids," a "closer contact" of the individual bishop with his flock, a more graceful method of "securing the retirement of an individual bishop when necessary."[17]

Edmund Hill, O.P., proposes a decentralization as extensive as that found in Anglo-American governments. In an essay on the development of institutions, Hill declares that Christ "did not, in my opinion, endow his Church with a constitution, with juridical institutions." Thinking at first that such a position is untenable, many will insist, says Hill, that "the papacy and the episcopacy are institutions *jure divino*, established personally by Christ." However, upon further reflection it becomes evident that there is a distinction between the establishment of a juridical authority and the establishment of a juridical institution. The fact that Jesus gave his Church authority to make laws doesn't mean that he insisted on the permanency of the institution through which it was first exercised. Hill puts it this way: "Authority cannot indeed be exercised except through an appropriate institution; but on the other hand the institution through which an authority is exercised is not necessarily the only possible or even the best institution for giving effect to that authority. An abiding authority therefore may be vested in a temporary institution." Supporting this position by analogy, Hill explains that although the authority of the English Navy is now exercised by

---

16 Hans Küng, "And After the Council?," *Commonweal* LXXX (September 3, 1965), 622.
17 Joseph O'Donohue, *Elections in the Church* (Baltimore: Helicon, 1967), pp. 41–54.

the Board of Admiralty, it was once exercised by the Lord High Admiral. This was a change from an individual to a commission, a change of institution but no change of authority. "As I see it," says Hill, "our Lord gave all the requisite authority to the Church, and the apostles, and Peter; but he left them to work out for themselves the juridical institutions necessary for exercising all this authority as might seem good to them and the Holy Spirit." Although granting that authority was given by Jesus to a visibly organized society, Hill says that "there is no need to conclude that its organization is more than temporary and provisional."[18]

Hill goes on to show how the exercise of authority in the Church *has* changed forms, becoming increasingly centralized. This increasing centralization is evident from the beginning of the Church up to the present time: from the "very first institution" the apostles devised—the most " 'democratic' possible"; to the "monarchical episcopate," when a "loose federation" of local Churches were each "ruled monarchically by its bishop"; to "federal institutions," i.e., regional synods, patriarchs, ecumenical councils; to the presidency of Leo the Great over an "ecumenical federation of local churches"; to the feudal suzerainty of the pope in the Middle Ages; to the absolutism of today, in which the pope is the "sole monarch" of a "unitary 'monolithic' monarchy," in which the "bishops have the effective status only of governors of provinces." If the message of the Second Vatican Council is to be applied, says Hill, the "absolutist concept of authority" must be supplanted by principles found in Anglo-American political institutions, namely, "those of representation, of the separation of powers, and of constitutional responsibility."[19]

According to Brian Tierney, theologians are once again recognizing the constitutional principle declared valid by the Council of Constance in the decree *Haec sancta,* enacted April 6, 1415. In effect, the Council of Constance subjects

---

18 Edmund Hill, O.P., "Authority in the Church: II. Development of Institutions," *Clergy Review,* L (September, 1965), 675–676.
19 *Ibid.,* 679.

the pope to the decrees of a council. The key passage reads as follows:

> This holy synod of Constance, constituting a general council and lawfully assembled to root out the present schism and to bring about the reform of the church in head and members . . . declares that, representing the Church militant, it holds its power immediately from Christ and that anyone of whatsoever state of dignity, even if it be the papal, is bound to obey it in matters which pertain to the faith, the rooting out of the said schism and the general reform of the church in head and members. Further it declares that any person of whatsoever rank, state or dignity, even if it be the papal, who contumaciously refuses to obey the statutes, mandates, ordinances or instructions made by this holy synod . . . or by any other general council lawfully assembled concerning the aforesaid matters shall be subjected to fitting penance and duly punished. . . .[20]

For four hundred years the validity of the Council of Constance was disputed. Then, says Tierney, after the establishment of the primacy of the papacy by the First Vatican Council, it came to be generally assumed by Catholic scholars "that *Haec sancta* was invalid and, moreover, that the principle affirmed in it was heretical. In accordance with this presupposition an appropriate account of the Great Schism was contrived."[21] Tierney is suggesting, therefore, that Catholics have for the better part of a century interpreted history to fit a premise that is false. However, the truth of the matter began coming to light in the 1960's when a "radical re-evaluation of the Council of Constance" was undertaken by numerous scholars, "including Congar, De Vooght, Fink, Küng, Jedin, and Franzen."[22] Hans Küng concluded, says Tierney, "that *Haec sancta* was a valid decree of a general council and binding on the Church for ever." Summarizing the thought of Humbert Jedin, Tierney maintains that since it was impossible to decide which of the three pontiffs was truly pope, "the real facts of the situation were that the schism could be ended

---

[20] Brian Tierney, "Roots of Western Constitutionalism in the Church's Own Tradition," *We, the People of God,* edited by James A. Coriden (Huntington, Ind.: Our Sunday Visitor Press, 1968), p. 120.
[21] *Ibid.,* p. 121.
[22] *Ibid.,* p. 122.

only by a decree asserting jurisdiction of the council over all three claimants. To deny the validity of the decree which declared this principle is to deny the validity of the only measure which proved capable of ending the schism."[23] Tierney then goes on to explain that medieval conciliarism failed to become the form of Church government, not because of any inherent incompatibility with Catholic doctrine, but because "Pope Eugene IV and his successors were determined it should fail."[24] Tierney also suggests that we profit from a mistake of the past and not repeat it. Since the principle of collegiality has recently been reasserted, we must set about reforming the structures which impede its full implementation. "The Council of Constance failed and the results of that failure were disastrous for the Church. We have another chance and we have less excuse for failing. We have not forgotten our history and we are not condemned to repeat it."[25]

Now the principle of subsidiarity implies that certain basic decisions (e.g., who should be placed in the papal office and how long he should serve) are properly those of a subsidiary level. And if the faithful in general have a modicum of understanding about such matters, these basic decisions ought to be made at the lowest level of subsidiarity, namely, by all the faithful. What this means is that the pope, though supreme, is still subject to the bishops and that the pope and bishops, though the legitimately constituted ruling authority in the Church, are still subject to the whole Church. In the previous chapter it was mentioned that a pope can be removed from office for such things as insanity, heresy, and schism. If the pope himself were to usurp the right to decide upon, say, his competency to remain in office (especially if his sanity were being questioned), the principle of subsidiarity would be violated. Such a decision obviously belongs to another—and therefore lower—level of authority, as there is no level equivalent to or higher than the pope's level. Now,

---

[23] Ibid., p. 123.
[24] Ibid., p. 126.
[25] Ibid., p. 128.

if the pope, who is supreme, is subject to the hierarchy for his continuance in office, the same kind of situation seems fitting (and theologically valid) between a bishop and the faithful in a diocese, or between the hierarchy in general and the faithful in general. For if the pope, who is supreme, is subject to the decision of a subsidiary level, for an even greater reason the bishops should be, as they are not supreme. And just as the hierarchy may assert itself against the pope for good reason (as it did at the Council of Constance), the laity may assert itself against the pope and bishops for good reason. What constitutes a good reason would be up to the laity to decide. But offhand one might suggest, as a good reason for the laity to assert itself, the chronic tendency of Church officers to be more concerned about the preservation of institutional status and personal power than about the human problems of poverty, racism, and war. The precise method by which the laity would assert itself effectively is not yet clear, but such things as the "Free Church" movement and periodic lay assemblies are distinct possibilities.

What has happened is that Catholics have generally interpreted the notion that the pope is supreme in such a way as to believe that he has the final word on every decision made in the Church. But if he possessed the right to review every decision, he would not only be supreme but absolute. It is not necessary that the pope have the right to review every decision in order to be supreme. Certainly the president of the United States is the supreme ruler. But he can be impeached. He is supreme, even though there are other powers that prevent him from becoming absolute, namely the judicial and legislative powers. Though supreme, he is subject to the constitution, the laws enacted by the legislature, the interpretations given by the courts, and the vote of the people, who may remove him from office. The supreme authority is simply the top authority, not the only authority. A chief executive, of the State or of the Church, can be supreme without having the right to decide how long he is to remain in office, or the right to make certain other basic decisions.

Catholics in general fail to recognize that some decisons in the Church belong by right to all the people, not merely the officials. At present, all final decisions go to the pope by default. Not aware of their rights, the faithful acquiesce in the usurpation of a basic right, namely, the right to decide who should be the chief executive of the Church and how long he should remain in office. Just because at present the people submit to a quasi-representative method of electing a pope or of allowing him to continue in office does not mean that the present system has to remain or that the present system is even desirable. It seems safe to conclude from the evidence of history that the decision as to whether the pope should remain in office is not included in the province of infallibility. The decision has usually been left to the pope, but the customs and laws which make this possible are not insurmountable. This is clear from the action of the bishops at the Council of Constance, which deposed three rival pontiffs. Now if it is the law which prevents the pope from being removed from office (or elected for a short term), then the situation can change. The binding force of a law depends upon the degree to which it secures the common good. If in fact a law violates the common good, there is no obligation to observe it. Such a law has no more force than an obsolete custom. If a law truly works against the common good, a person has the right and the duty to expose and to eradicate it.

If the decision as to whether the pope should continue in office belongs to the faithful, then every decision of the pope, in effect, is subject to the review and approval of the faithful. For if the faithful are convinced that a particular decision of the pope is gravely detrimental to the common good, they could insist that he reverse his decision or simply remove him from office. Of course, under the present system there is no way to accomplish such a thing. Changes would have to be introduced into the system to enable the fatihful to exercise their right in such a matter.

No doubt some would question whether the faithful possess the right to determine who should serve as chief executive and how long he should serve. However, the faithful do have such a right, as is evident from the nature of government and the nature of the Church's mission. It is clear from the evolvement of Anglo-American political theory that every person possesses certain inalienable rights, that governments are instituted to protect and to secure these rights, and that when government works against the attainment of this end it may be altered or a new form of government established. Such, in brief, is the argument from the nature of government.

The argument from the mission of the Church is as follows. The principle of subsidiarity implies that the final decision of a juridical or executive or legislative matter rests ultimately with the faithful. This flows from the fact that the purpose of the Church is to help mankind realize its full potential. But the laity, as such, are directly in touch with the condition of man and best able therefore to reflect his most pressing needs, to which the Church should minister. Therefore, decisions which affect the condition of man (and this means practically all Church decisions in one way or another) ought to be subject ultimately to the review of the faithful, at least to the extent of replacing the chief executive of the Church periodically. The laity are the principal vehicle by which the Church contributes to the personal and social fulfillment of man. Not to allow them to exercise the right to decide who will be the chief executive of the Church is to violate the principle of subsidiarity.

If necessary, the laity must take matters into their own hands. What happened at the Council of Constance was that the bishops recognized the need for reform and organized their power in an attempt to achieve reform. A similar thing must happen today, if the principle of subsidiarity is to be fully applied. The laity must assert their power by organizing to democratize the Church.

If the hierarchy would attempt to suppress the formation of independent groups working toward the democratization of the Church, they would, in effect, be acting contrary to their own teachings. The Council Fathers declared the right of the laity to organize in the Decree on the Apostolate of the Laity. Speaking of the "great variety of associations in the apostolate," the bishops said that the "laity have the right to found and run such associations and to join those already existing" (n. 19).[26] Further, the right of the laity to organize is implicit in the social teachings of the Church. The laity have as much right to organize to protect their common interests as do other groups.

The American layman may be the lever needed to supply the extra pressure that will move the Church away from medieval structures of government. He is not, by and large, vocationally dependent upon the Church. He has cultivated a distinct preference for democracy, being a product of American society. He is fairly well educated and rather secure. In a greater or lesser measure, he has heard the call for freedom issued by men like Novak, Callahan, DuBay, Groppi, Rahner, Schillebeeckx, Küng, O'Hanlon, Riga, Haring, Murray, Baum, and McKenzie. Things have changed, says Callahan: "The new freedom is here to stay. Not all the condemnations that any anxious pope or bishop could pronounce, nor any new Syllabus of Errors or Neo-Modernist oath, could make more than a momentary difference." Callahan is convinced that laws and pressures from those in power in the Church would have little effect in present circumstances: "The new freedom is a genuine movement of the people, springing from a sudden and wholly unexpected vision of what the Church can become, of what it must no longer be. The vision is cloudy, the efforts fumbling. Yet there is power and life."[27] Callahan points out that groups at odds with the Church power structure have found an ally in the public press, which is always eager for data on tense situations. A group with a serious viewpoint vigorously held can no longer be silenced. *Ad hoc* groups and protest movements are apt to be a continuing feature of American Catholic life.[28]

It would seem, however, that if democracy is to become a

---

26 Abbott, *op. cit.*, pp. 509–510.
27 Callahan, "The New Freedom," *loc. cit.*, p. 405.
28 Daniel Callahan, "Preparing for Diversity," *Commonweal*, LXXXII (September 24, 1965), 696.

reality in the Church, great numbers of the People of God would ultimately be needed to help organize toward this end. A massive movement is needed. Whether such a movement can take place depends upon more than the inspiration of a few charismatic leaders or the witness of a few protest groups. Much depends upon whether the time is ripe. Here it will be helpful to draw upon the sociological data of the civil rights movement. If mass community action in the civil rights area will produce legal and institutional changes in secular society, it is reasonable to assume that a diocesan, national, or international ground swell of the laity would produce legal and institutional changes in the Church. The late sociologist Robert B. Johnson lists six ingredients for mass community action. To the degree these are present in the Church, to this degree is the Church ripe for a ground swell for a democratic Church. The six ingredients are as follows:

1) An *ideal*—a philosophical or theological base . . .
2) A sense of *threat,* or of outside pressure from a dominant group . . .
3) A *symbol*—a rallying point which symbolizes discrimination . . .
4) A semi-independent *leadership structure,* whose hands are not tied by the dominant group . . .
5) A medium of *communication* . . .
6) An awareness of *extra-community influences,* or sources of emotional, financial and advisory supports from outside the community.[29]

Let us see, now, whether these ingredients are to be found among the People of God in the United States. The *ideal* is democracy, which Americans instinctively support because of their political heritage. Scholars like Peter Riga and John L. McKenzie are proclaiming the virtues of democracy as a means of achieving the freedom that belongs to the People of God. The documents of Vatican II make bold statements about freedom being a personal and inalienable right. These statements may spark a drive to exercise that freedom democratically.

---

[29] Robert Johnson, "The Changing Status of the Negro in American Life," Report submitted to the NAIRO consultative conference, January 21, 1960, p. 14.

The sense of *threat* is present in many ways. Any creative person who has undertaken novel projects in the Roman Catholic Church has more than likely felt the heavy, restraining hand of authority. The monarchical form of government in itself provides a sense of threat in today's world. In addition, a sense of threat arises from the silence of the Church in the face of such massive problems as race, poverty, war, population, and technology. At any moment these problems may explode in a nuclear holocaust.

The *symbol* is present in Jesus himself, who was constantly fighting the discrimination of the religious establishment of his time, and in many of the saints. Joan of Arc, for example, brings to mind the extreme malice of which those in power are capable. Further, she reminds us not only of discrimination against the laity in general, but of that against women in particular. In the Roman Catholic Church women have been the object of intense discrimination.

A *semi-independent leadership* exists among the laity who are professionally and economically secure. More than 100,000 Catholics graduate each year from secular campuses alone, not to mention the Catholic schools. Bright, articulate, determined, these Catholics are a more independent breed than the immigrant of several generations ago.

The *medium of communication* exists in such publications as the *National Catholic Reporter,* the *Critic,* and the *Commonweal,* as well as the secular communications media. A little ingenuity generates extensive coverage. Key issues can be kept visible by dramatic action. Here the civil rights demonstrators have provided a pattern that might be used occasionally. As theology and public opinion develop, dramatic action can become more bold.

The *extra-community resources* involve groups of like-minded people in other areas. For example, a local affiliate of the National Association of Laymen has support from other affiliates and from the national organization as well. The National Committee on Catholic Concerns is another organization that would provide extra-community support. In one way or another, practically every group working toward freedom would be a support. Civil rights groups, political groups like ADA, ecumenical religious groups—all of these might be able to offer help in specific cases.

Apparently, conditions in the United States are fairly ripe for the beginning of a ground swell toward a democratic form of Church government. The laymen have an unusual opportunity to take the lead in catalyzing such a movement. In doing so, the laymen will not only promote their own freedom, but they will also strengthen the Church as a whole. A more widespread distribution of power would mean, in effect, a larger aggregate of power for the achievement of the Church's purposes.

It is clear by now that the principle of subsidiarity inheres in Catholic teaching, that the laity have the power to implement it in a fuller way, and that such an implementation will increase the power of the Church to achieve its mission. Because the principle of subsidiarity inheres in the teaching of the Roman Catholic Church, democracy is a possible form of Church government. Because monarchy is slow to achieve subsidiarity, democracy is a more desirable form of Church government. Subsidiarity is, in effect, a rationale for a democratic Church. Although it is theoretically possible to have an adequate number and the proper kinds of subsidiary structures in a monarchy, in practice there tends to be an enormous lag between what is needed and what is developed.

Five hundred years after the Council of Constance, the Roman Catholic Church is still without a constitutional form of government, even though such a form has proven helpful to other Churches and to secular governments. The officials at the Vatican, and even the thousands of bishops in the world, do not have the vision that is required to recognize far enough in advance the kinds of subsidiary structures that will be needed to help mankind fulfill itself. Nor do they have the expertise that is needed to establish such structures in adequate number. Further, it is not likely that the people who use the structures will be satisfied with them if they do not have a hand in shaping them. With social relations multiply-ing, it is more important than ever before that new structures arise as they are needed. This requires a flexibility that seems to be practically impossible with monarchy. Democracy alone seems to offer the necessary flexibility.

CHAPTER IX

THE PROPHETIC PRINCIPLE

An obstacle to the democratization of the Roman Catholic Church may arise from the misuse of bureaucratic power. The administrative structure of the Church could be used to stifle initiative that might lead to a democratic Church. A docile laity, some would argue, could not be expected to sustain a power drive against the bureaucracy. In a bureaucracy, changes must come from the top, as that is where the power lies. But those in power are not apt to surrender their power willingly; they are not apt to allow democratization to go very far. Such a line of reasoning does not take into account the many dimensions of the Church. The Church is more than a bureaucracy (which in itself is a good thing). The Church is primarily a charismatic community and only secondarily a bureaucracy. The bureaucracy exists for the sake of the People of God, most of whom are not part of the bureaucracy, most of whom are not employed by the Church. The charismatic dimension of the Church includes prophetic utterance, which serves as a counterbalance to bureaucracy. The excesses of bureaucracy can be held in check by those who are not economically and vocationally dependent upon the Church, if they respond adequately to prophetic impulses from the Spirit. While a prophet may arise from within the bureaucracy, he is usually removed from it if the bureaucracy is seriously deformed and if it is the object of his denunciation. Those who are not vocationally and economically dependent on the Church have no vested interest in being silent about the evils that tend to develop in bureaucratic structures of the Church. Those who are not part of the vocational structure of the Church tend to have a more objective point of view and a greater freedom to expose inconsistencies and to insist on reform. Being outside the bureaucracy, the prophet has a power that cannot be suppressed by the customary power plays of bureaucrats. Prophetic utterance can alter public opinion, rouse the masses, and predispose the Church for institutional change that could lead to democracy.

The above paragraph provides a brief outline of the key ideas in this chapter. It is now appropriate to examine bureaucracy and prophecy in greater detail. First of all, it should be noted that bureaucracy can be a very useful instrument for achieving the objectives of government, both in the State and in the Church. The more complex government becomes, the more necessary is bureaucracy. It can be expected that in the decades ahead, bureaucracy will occupy an even greater position of importance than it does at present. According to Peter Woll, the growth of bureaucracy should not be viewed with alarm: "It adds an important new dimension to our government. American bureaucracy takes its place as an equal partner with the President, Congress, and the Judiciary. Its existence not only increases the ability of our government to meet the challenges of the twentieth century, but also enhances the meaning of constitutional democracy."[1] McKenzie discusses bureaucracy in relation to the Church. After warning against its dangers, he commends its use in moderation: "The Church has grown to vast proportions and engages in a complex variety of activities. . . . In order to manage this immense machinery, bureaucracy is the necessary instrument."[2]

---

[1] Cited by Frederick C. and John M. Dyer, *Bureaucracy Vs. Creativity* (Coral Gables, Florida: University of Miami Press, 1965), p. 20.
[2] McKenzie, *Authority in the Church,* p. 144.

However, if bureaucracy is overextended, it can be an obstacle to creative growth. According to Marshall E. Dimock, bureaucracy is the opposite of enterprise. Bureaucracy, on the one hand, involves "routine, security, method, stability, group decision, undeviating procedure, monopoly." Enterprise, on the other hand, involves "innovation, risk-taking, drive, constant change, individual initiative, flexible adjustment to change, competition."[3] What Philip Scharper wrote even before the Second Vatican Council ended is worth recalling today: "The sociologists point out . . . that if there is to be any significant change (other than revolution) in an organization, the change must come from the top." Both Pope John and Pope Paul issued appeals for reform, and the Council charted the basic direction of change and laid down guidelines for some specific changes. "But none of this," says Scharper, "will really make much difference in those places where authority is still authoritarian."[4]

Much of what passes for reform is authoritarianism in disguise. Eugene B. Jennings describes a phenomenon called "bu-reaction," which he says is more widespread than is generally realized. Bu-reaction is "almost always accompanied by a burst of emotional vitality." It is the clamor of a "bu-reactor," someone who "stands within the bureaucracy shouting about wanting to get out, but never making any attempt to get out." A bu-reactor vents his anger on red tape, conservatism, bureaucracy, and other scapegoats. Then he is able to "return to his bureaucratic style, feeling that he is really not a bureaucrat after all." The bu-reactor develops "a sense of prestige and identity by ranting judiciously against the system. Yet he violates none of the sacred rituals and taboos." According to Jennings, "the bu-reactor is quite common today."[5]

If Pope Paul VI grows progressively conservative, or if the

---

[3] Marshall E. Dimock, *A Philosophy of Administration toward Creative Growth* (New York: Harper & Brothers Publishers, 1958), p. 162.
[4] Philip Scharper, "Is It Time to Overhaul the Pyramidical Structure of Authority in the Church?," *Critic,* XXIII (October-November, 1964), 39.
[5] Cited by Dyer, *op. cit.,* p. 26.

next pope is an authoritarian, the vast bureaucracy of the Church can be turned against renewal. All the bureaucrats and bu-reactors up and down the line can become agents of retrogression. Bureaucrats prefer patience to prophecy. Exceptional priests (like William H. DuBay of Los Angeles and James E. Groppi of Milwaukee) become prophetic when permissiveness prevails. But when authoritarianism is dominant for a long period of time, prophetic personalities seldom emerge from a bureaucracy. In such a period, prophets usually arise from outside the bureaucracy, though there are always exceptions.

Max Weber wrote that the Roman Catholic Church is a rather distinctly developed bureaucracy, "increasingly so since the end of the thirteenth century."[6] The frightening thing about bureaucracy is this: "Once it is fully established, bureaucracy is among those social structures which are the hardest to destroy." Furthermore, "where the bureaucratization of administration has been completely carried through, a form of power relation is established that is practically unshatterable."[7] Those who wield power in a bureaucracy are confined by their position: "The individual bureaucrat cannot squirm out of the apparatus in which he is harnessed." And those who are caught at the bottom of the power structure cannot "dispense with or replace the bureaucratic apparatus of authority once it exists."[8] It would seem, then, that the Roman Catholic Church is subject to the whims and fancies of the hierarchy. When it is expedient the hierarchy can allow a certain measure of democratization, but when their power is threatened they can quickly revert to authoritarian practices by utilizing the powerful bureaucratic structures at their disposal.

Fortunately, however, there is more to the Church than bureaucracy. The Church has a prophetic principle that tends to correct bureaucratic dysfunctions. Were all members of

---

[6] *From Max Weber: Essays in Sociology,* ed. and trans. H. H. Gerth and C. Wright Mills (New York: Oxford University Press, 1958), p. 204.
[7] *Ibid.,* p. 228.
[8] *Ibid.,* p. 229.

the Church part of the bureaucracy, the principle might never be activated. But most members of the Church are not part of the bureaucracy. Those who are economically and vocationally dependent upon the bureaucracy (clergy, religious, salaried lay teachers, etc.) may be generally incapable of responding dramatically to prophetic impulses. But others (the majority of the laity) often will be free to respond to such impulses from the Spirit. They will be free to expose what the bureaucrat prefers to keep silent. The vivid proclamation of truth by prophetic laymen can help to prune the bureaucratic tree of excessive growth.

A prophet may be described as one who speaks for God. He is a mouthpiece for God. In a sense, everyone is called to prophecy: "I will pour out my Spirit upon all flesh: and your sons and your daughters shall prophesy."[9] But prophecy admits of degree. Some are called to more extreme forms of prophecy than others. Not every prophet is as dramatic as Ezekiel or as moving as Amos or as caustic as Jesus. A prophet may be as sophisticated as John F. Kennedy or as shrill as James E. Groppi. The right to free speech provides an objective justification for the exercise of the prophetic principle. The impulse from the Spirit provides the subjective motivation. And just as the personalities of the prophets differ, so also do the kinds of prophetic utterance. Some apply to the future, some to the abuses in the social order, and some to the abuses in the Church. This chapter is primarily concerned with the prophetic utterances that apply to abuses within the Church, specifically the abuses of authority. Inasmuch as this kind of prophecy is seldom understood by Catholics, it will be in order to discuss it at some length. We now turn to a discussion of free speech and then to a description of the kind of prophecy that is capable of neutralizing bureaucratic excesses.

The Constitution on the Church says that the layman should speak out, that he has a duty to make his voice heard:

---

[9] Acts 2:17.

"An individual layman . . . is permitted and sometimes even obliged to express his opinion on things which concern the good of the Church" (n. 37).[10] Pius XII openly proclaimed the need for free speech in the Church. Rahner cites a talk given by Pius XII to the International Catholic Press Congress and carried in the *Osservatore Romano* of February 18, 1950: "Public opinion plays a part in every normal society of human beings . . . wherever there is no expression of public opinion, above all, where it has been ascertained that no public opinion exists, then one is obliged to say that there is a fault, a weakness, a sickness, in the social life of that area." Pius XII goes on to speak about public opinion within the Church: "She too is a living body, and there would be something missing from her life if there were no public opinion within her, a defect for which pastors as well as the faithful would be responsible."[11]

Rahner says that public opinion exists within the Church to make clear what the faithful are really believing. Church leaders depend upon it to know the real situation. How else are the leaders to be informed about what needs to be changed, improved, or developed in the Church, says Rahner, unless there is a free expression of likes and dislikes? Even the person who apparently has nothing to say must be given opportunity to talk himself out in order that the reactions of others may be witnessed.[12] Rahner insists that the life of the Church is sustained, not by the initiative of the hierarchy alone, but by that of the laity as well. The laity are especially disposed to respond to the Spirit and to speak as they are moved.[13] Muller quotes a talk given by Rahner during the *Austrian Katholikentag* at Salzburg in 1962: "The laity must speak up and openly proclaim their opinion, even before the Church authorities, even if they make a nuisance of them-

---

10 Abbott, *op. cit.*, p. 64.
11 Karl Rahner, S.J., *Free Speech in the Church* (New York: Sheed and Ward, 1959), p. 14.
12 *Ibid.*, p. 21.
13 *Ibid.*, p. 18.

selves, . . . even if they are misjudged or even punished."[14]
Writing on the relationship between nature and grace, Rahner
says that grace poured out by the Spirit is not always perceived
as grace. A person, therefore, need not wait for a miracle
before he acts on his feelings and opinions. Says Rahner:
"In practice we cannot clearly distinguish grace from the level
of spiritual-personal individuality, which in itself still belongs
to the natural sphere, even though it works itself out in the
religious sphere too."[15]

Besides Rahner, many other Catholic thinkers write about
the need for public opinion and free speech within the Church.
Schillebeeckx declares that "there is a place in the Church
for 'public opinion' and open discussion in which the layman
may put forward his own point of view." It is not simply in
worldly matters that the layman has "a right to intervene
both by word and action," but also in "whatever concerns the
salvation of mankind."[16] McKenzie, recognizing that elected
officials in the modern democratic state cannot afford to be
unaware of public opinion, states that Church officials have
an even greater reason for encouraging and knowing public
opinion—it is a channel for the influence of the Holy Spirit.[17]
Public opinion, argues McKenzie, is meaningful only if it
reviews and criticizes authority. Democracy shows that public
opinion may contribute to a peaceful community, for people
are more apt to abide by laws they have helped (through the
expression of public opinion) to make.[18] Daniel Callahan
writes that it is time to stop "speaking with bated breath,
with thoughts deliberately concealed." Direct speech is to be
the consequence, he says, of the "strong winds of the Second
Vatican Council."[19] Callahan takes cognizance of the hierar-

---

[14] Karl Rahner, S.J., *Orientierieng,* XXVI (1962), 134, quoted in Alois
Muller, *Obedience in the Church,* p. 156.
[15] Karl Rahner, S.J., *Nature and Grace* (New York: Sheed and Ward,
1964), p. 33.
[16] Schillebeeckx, *The Layman in the Church,* p. 51.
[17] McKenzie, *Authority in the Church,* p. 180.
[18] *Ibid.,* p. 171.
[19] Daniel Callahan (ed.), *Generation of the Third Eye* (New York: Sheed
and Ward, 1965), p. 5.

chy's tendency to be offended by candid expression and to question the loyalty of laymen who disagree with them. He suggests that bishops ought to learn that disagreement is not disloyalty.[20] Hans Küng writes that the virtue of prudence has been misunderstood. Prudence is not to be equated with the utterance of what authorities want to hear; instead, it means "frankness that feels no embarrassment" and "boldness that has no fear," as when "Paul 'withstood Peter to the face' (Gal. 2:11)." The Catholic Church today is still in a defensive position from the challenge of the "Reformation, Gallicanism, the Enlightenment, the French Revolution, Liberalism, and Socialism." Hence, too often, because of an excessive defensiveness, caution rather than courage has been the by-word. But the courageous Christian speaks boldly: "The witness of freedom of speech in the Church has been borne by Irenaeus against Pope Victor, Jerome against Damasus, Columban against Boniface IV, Bernard of Clairvaux against Eugene III, Bridget of Sweden against Gregory II, Philip Neri against Clement III; and by so many other saints like Catherine of Siena, Thomas More, Robert Bellarmine." It was Thomas Aquinas who insisted upon the right of free criticism, not only of one's peers, but even of one's superiors. And it was Gregory the Great who said that "if scandal is taken at the truth, it is better to allow scandal to arise than to neglect the truth."[21]

Having examined a few remarks about free speech in general, we now turn to a discussion of prophecy, a particular kind of free speech. The Constitution on the Church states: "Christ, the great Prophet . . . continually fulfills His prophetic office . . . not only through the hierarchy . . . but also through the laity" (n. 35).[22] Pope John speaks of the power that is made available through contact with the Spirit: "The divine Redeemer promised us a gift from heaven. He prom-

20 Daniel Callahan, *The Mind of the Catholic Layman* (New York: Charles Scribner's Sons, 1963), p. 141.
21 Küng, *Freedom Today*, pp. 57–58.
22 Abbott, *op. cit.*, p. 61.

ised, that is, to send us the Paraclete, the Holy Spirit, from
the bosom of the Father. 'You will receive power,' He said,
'when the Spirit comes upon you' Acts 1:8."[23] The *New
Catholic Encyclopedia* says: "The prophetical office of the
layman is an immediate consequence of the Sacrament of
Confirmation. . . . Some, because of natural endowments, particular charisms, and circumstances of life will be engaged
in a more articulate exercise of their prophetical commission; . . . special graces and charisms (1 Pt 4:10) are bestowed upon individuals for renewal and building up of the
Church."[24]

Prophets are indispensable for the renewal of the Church.
Says McKenzie: "The prophet is the means by which the
Spirit protects the Church against corruption. . . . The Spirit
often speaks to the officers of the Church through those whom
the officers govern; if the officers do not hear the voice of the
Spirit from this source, they will not hear it at all."[25] In a
chapter on "The Prophetic Office" McKenzie acknowledges
that the prophet (like the bishop) is not always without fault
or excess. But if bishops are not removed from office for
mistakes, the prophets should have some kind of immunity
as well. However, "the ugly fact is that Church authority can
suppress prophets, and prophets cannot suppress Church authority." The suppression of prophets seems to be an automatic
reaction on the part of authority. What accounts for such a
phenomenon? According to McKenzie, suppression of the
prophets by authority occurs because the prophet, who is
inspired by the Spirit, cannot be controlled: "The prophet
speaks with an assurance which is not given him by Church
authority; he may be as obedient and submissive as one could
desire, but so long as he is a prophet, he cannot be managed.
The prophet remains outside the structure of official authority."
Although the prophet is necessary for the work of Church

---

[23] John XXIII, "Meditations for the Council," *The Pope Speaks,* VIII
(Autumn, 1962), 135.
[24] "Theology of the Laity," *New Catholic Encyclopedia* (New York: Mc-
Graw-Hill Book Company, 1967), VIII, 329.
[25] McKenzie, "Authority and Power in the New Testament," *op. cit.,* p. 420.

renewal, his course is not an easy one: "If one wants to be a prophet, one must think of oneself as expendable."[26]

Bruce Vawter, known for his scholarship on the Old Testament prophets, points out that the prophets were always saying something that authorities did not want to hear. Although the prophet preached the traditional beliefs, there was always something radical about his message. According to Vawter, recent studies emphasize the all-important truth "that however dependent the prophet was on Israelite tradition and however he may have stood in the mainstream of its religion, he was always first and foremost a charismatic character and his word was always 'New.' "[27]

What has been said above certainly dispels the notion that the Church is a peaceful community devoid of conflict. Not all disturbances in the household of the Faith are diabolical in origin. Some are from the Spirit. Peace is not to be maintained by authority at the expense of prophetic witness. Vincent F. Blehl, S.J., writes: "If the faithful are expected to obey their ecclesiastical superiors exercising juridical power, so also the hierarchy must become responsive to the Spirit in the faithful when the latter exercise their charismatic authority, the authority of conscience and truth."[28] Conflict in the Church is not to be despised. It is a prerequisite for reform and growth. There is a need, says Bishop Wright, for tension between conscience and authority. He praises Joan of Arc for her fidelity to conscience against the abuses of Church authority. He recognizes that polarity arises out of tension and ultimately produces harmony. He discusses the polarity that exists in art, in physics, in drama, in music, in biology, and life. Without a certain tension in life, "there is no harmony or health."[29] An admirer of Newman, Wright quotes a passage

---

[26] McKenzie, *Authority in the Church*, pp. 157–158.
[27] Bruce Vawter, "Recent Literature on the Prophets," *The Human Reality of Sacred Scripture*, ed. Pierre Benoit, O.P., and Roland E. Murphy, O. Carm., Vol. X of *Concilium*, ed. Edward H. Schillebeeckx, O.P., *et al.* (New York: Paulist Press, 1965), p. 124.
[28] Vincent F. Blehl, S.J., "The Council: A Lesson from the Past," *America,* CVII (October 27, 1962), 952.
[29] Wright, "Reflections on Conscience and Authority," *loc. cit.,* p. 28.

from the *Apologia pro Vita Sua,* which shows that conflict is part of the Church: Catholic Christendom, says Newman, "is a vast assemblage of human beings with wilful intellects and wild passions, brought together into one by the beauty and the majesty of a superhuman power."[30] Alfred North White-head sees conflict as an integral part of society, flowing from liberty and resting on a metaphysical principle. Says White-head in *The Adventure of Ideas:* "Every occasion of actuality is in its own nature finite. There is no totality which is the harmony of all perfections. Whatever is realized in any one occasion of experience necessarily excludes the unbounded welter of contrary possibilities." Whitehead goes on to say that "this doctrine is a commonplace in fine arts. It is—or should be—a commonplace of political philosophy. History can only be understood by seeing it as the theatre of diverse groups of idealists urging ideals incompatible for joint reali-zation."[31]

Conflict in the Church is the natural concomitant of the interplay between the hierarchical and the prophetic princi-ples. They serve both as power checks and action stimulants. The value of the institution has long been recognized by Catholics, but the value of prophecy has not been perceived quite so clearly. Bernard G. Murchland, C.S.C., sees the pro-phetic principle as a "counterweight to the institutional." The institution may be blind to certain sufferings, but the prophet can see. Says Murchland: "Frightful is the agony of man; no human voice can convey its full terror. Prophecy is the voice God has lent to the silent agony, a voice of the plundered poor, to the profaned riches of the world. It is a form of living, a crossing point of God and man. God is raging in the prophetic words."[32] When the prophet rages, authority tends to listen, even though its responses are not always favorable to the prophet.

---

[30] *Ibid.,* p. 25.
[31] Cited by Bernard Martin, "Force and Persuasion: Alfred North White-head's Philosophy of History," *Ohio University Review,* VIII (1966), 39.
[32] Bernard C. Murchland, C.S.C., "The Prophetic Principle," *Commonweal.* LXXXIV (April 29, 1966), 172.

Conflict between the institution and the prophet makes possible an honest dialogue. Dialogue is not possible with a paternalistic institution, for paternalism has no ears. Both sides must listen if there is to be dialogue. As Gregory Baum sees it, the Church today is situated in a dialogical context and will grow only if it engages in dialogue.[33] Martin Buber says that distance is a precondition for entering into relation and for unfolding the world of "the between," the world that has meaning. Ontologically, says Buber, there must be a movement toward distance before there can be an entering into relation and dialogue.[34] Within the Church, movement toward distance may be viewed as movement into prophecy.

Unfortunately, prophecy has been played down so long in Catholicism that its most potent forms are often mistaken for something diabolical. A weak image of prophecy prevails. There have, of course, been prophetic utterances by saints against authority, but these are seldom quoted in the pulpit. The average Catholic, consequently, has a distorted view of some of the saints.

The language of the prophet is sometimes quite shocking. He is not afraid to say things that offend polite society. Thus, the prophet Amos can speak as follows: "Hear this word, you cows of Bashan."[35] And the prophet Malachi can scandalize the clergy: "And now, O priests, this command is for you. If you will not listen . . . says the Lord of hosts, then I will send the curse upon you and I will curse your blessings . . . I will rebuke your offspring and spread dung upon your face."[36] But Jesus was the most caustic of all the prophets in relation to abuses of authority by religious leaders. The strongest language placed upon the lips of Jesus is found in the twenty-third chapter of the Gospel of Matthew, in which Jesus ac-

---

[33] Gregory Baum, O.S.A., "Restlessness in the Church," *Ecumenist,* V (March-April, 1967), 33.
[34] Martin Buber, *Knowledge of Man,* ed. Maurice Friedman, trans. Maurice Friedman and Ronald Gregor (New York: Harper & Row, Publishers, 1965), pp. 52–71.
[35] Amos 4:1.
[36] Malachi 2:1–3.

cuses the scribes and Pharisees of hypocrisy. Apparently, Jesus believed the scribes made too much of the law, and was calling them to account for it. But the average Catholic, conditioned never to criticize Church authorities, would hardly associate the scribes and Pharisees with those in the Roman Catholic bureaucracy who make too much of the law. The average Catholic would never see this passage as a prophetic utterance against the authoritarianism and paternalism characteristic of many bishops and priests. Yet there is definitely a parallel. To understand this kind of prophecy it might be helpful to select a few paragraphs from the twenty-third chapter of Matthew and substitute the words "bishops and priests" for the words "scribes and Pharisees." The Prophet Jesus said:

> The scribes and Pharisees . . . bind heavy burdens, hard to bear, and lay them on men's shoulders; but they will not lift their finger. . . .
> But woe to you, hypocrites! for you cleanse the outside of the cup and of the plate, but inside they are full of extortion and rapacity. . . .
> Woe to you, hypocrites! for you are like whitewashed tombs, which outwardly appear righteous to man, but within you are full of dead men's bones and all uncleanness. . . .
> Woe to you, for you build the tombs of prophets. . . . You serpents, you brood of vipers, how are you to escape being sentenced to hell? . . .[37]

But is it not absurd to maintain that a prophet might be called upon today to utter such vitriolic statements toward the hierarchy? Such utterances may have been applicable to popes and bishops of earlier times, but hardly today, it would seem. Members of the hierarchy have their faults, even their sins. But they confess and repent. This much can be granted. However, the sins that are recognized are not the ones that the prophet is chiefly concerned about. The prophet sees the sins that are not evident to those in authority, such sins as authoritarianism, racism, anti-semitism, discrimination against women, and silence in the face of immense human suffering.

Commenting on the conflict between Jesus and the scribes

---

[37] Matthew 23:2–33.

and Pharisees, Gregory Baum says that "the struggle of Jesus with the institution of his day reveals to us the condition of the Gospel in the world and the blindness which threatens the Christian Church." Just as Jesus was in conflict with the religious establishment of his time, the prophet of today is in conflict with the religious establishment of our time. "In other words," says Baum, "the struggle of Christ with the religious institution to which he belonged has ecclesiological significance. . . . Strangely enough, few theologians have focused their attention on the passage from old to new covenant, and the transition from Synagogue to Church, as an element in the understanding of redemption. It seems to me that in this transition, as presented in the New Testament, we have a revealed basis for a theology of social change. There we learn what is operative in the reform of institutional life and what are the forces that oppose it."[38] Therefore, the prophet is to be considered an indispensable agent of Church renewal. Church authorities cannot control him. He speaks the truth, whether it is convenient to do so or not. The pressures that work to keep bureaucrats quiet so that they may remain in their positions have no effect on the prophet. The fact is that the prophet is commissioned by God to point out the defects and the social sins of those in power, even to the point of using hostility.

But it would seem to some that the prophet should view the hierarchy as Christ viewed the adulterous woman, saying nothing about her sins. This is Rahner's image of the repentant Church, and the bureaucrats probably like it. But two things must not be overlooked in this image of the Church—the woman was repentant and she represented the whole Church. It is an entirely different situation when the hierarchy does not even recognize its sins of omission and its authoritarianism, i.e., when the hierarchy acts as if it is *the* Church. A precondition for forgiveness is repentance. A bishop will not

[38] Gregory Baum, *The Credibility of the Church Today: A Reply to Charles Davis* (New York: Herder and Herder, 1968), p. 66.

forgive an unrepentant sinner in the confessional. The prophet
should not be expected to forgive an unrepentant hierarchy.
If anything, the prophet ought to become more caustic, so
that the bishops will ultimately see their sins and finally be
moved to repentance. The prophet must proclaim the word
of God as he is moved by the Spirit. Here the dialogue between God and Isaiah is helpful, because it underlines the
intransigence of the prophet:

> Go, and say to this people:
>   "Hear and hear, but do not understand;
>   see and see, but do not perceive,"
>   Make the heart of this people fat,
>   and their ears heavy,
>   and shut their eyes;
>   lest they see with their eyes,
>   and hear with their ears,
>   and understand with their hearts,
>   and turn and be healed.
>   Then I said, "How long, O Lord?"
> And he said:
>   "Until cities lie waste
>   without inhabitant,
>   and houses without men,
>   and the land is utterly desolate. . . ."[39]

The point here is that even though God and the prophet
know that it is futile to speak to some people, the prophet
must continue to speak.

In short, prophetic utterance is an effective means of pin-
pointing bureaucratic dysfunctions. Bureaucratic power may
be invincible within the context of bureaucracy, but the
Church is more than a bureaucracy. The power balance includes all the People of God, some of whom are called to
extreme forms of prophetic witness. When the Spirit moves
a person to prophesy, power comes upon him and he speaks
with the authority of God. Increased authoritarianism may
curtail prophetic utterance from those who prefer to remain
within the bureaucratic structure of the Church, but it does not
have the same effect on those whose vocations lie in the sec-

[39] Isaiah 6:9–11.

ular world. An increase in authoritarianism might well increase the number of prophetic laymen. These in turn might provide the occasion for a great surge by other laymen toward a democratic Church. While prophecy does not lead necessarily to democracy, those promoting democracy can use prophecy as a means of removing bureaucratic obstacles that stand in the way of a democratic Church.

Because the Church is bureaucratic it ought to be democratic. If monarchy tends toward efficiency, it does so today because of a bureaucratic structure. But whereas monarchy needs bureaucracy if it is to function well, the reverse is not true. Bureaucracy does not need monarchy. Bureaucracy can work just as well, if not better, in a democracy. The need for efficiency in Church government is not an argument for monarchy; it is an argument for bureaucracy. And since bureaucracy can function just as well in a democracy as in a monarchy, the need for efficiency is *not* an argument against democracy. Further, because in a democracy leaders can more easily be removed, the bureaucracy itself is more under the control of the entire community. And because the purpose of bureaucracy is to serve the whole community, it would seem that bureaucracy would be better able to achieve its purposes in a democracy than in a monarchy.

Democracy is also desirable because of the prophetic nature of the Church. In other words, the prophetic principle is a rationale for the democratization of the Church. Being primarily a charismatic community, the Church should be a school for prophecy. In general, there is not enough said about the prophetic spirit in the Roman Catholic Church, at least about the extreme forms of prophecy. The officials of the Church may, in certain cases, tolerate prophetic utterance, as was the case with Archbishop Cousins and Father Groppi in Milwaukee. But more often prophecy is suppressed, as was the case with Cardinal McIntyre and Father DuBay in Los Angeles. The prophetic character of the Church needs to be set forth in more meaningful terms by the magisterium. It is not enough to say that the magisterium is the prophetic voice of Christ—this is an ordinary form of prophecy. It has to be said that people like Groppi and DuBay are also prophetic voices of Christ. Even though the hierarchy may not recognize Groppi and DuBay as prophets (the hierarchy may be the last to recognize a prophet), at least the hierarchy should recognize and teach that the prophets include all types of personalities.

The attitude toward prophets today is similar to that toward freedom prior to the Second Vatican Council. Freedom was tolerated when it was expedient, but truth seemed to be more important. The Second Vatican Council recognized the primacy of freedom in declaring it a personal and inalienable right. It is not something, therefore, to be tolerated, but something to be protected at all costs. Prophecy is not something that is simply to be tolerated either. Because it is essential to the well-being of the Church, prophecy must be promoted vigorously. But a monarchy of its very nature seems less inclined than democracy to encourage prophecy.

While prophets will appear under any form of government, it seems that more will develop in a democracy. For in a democracy there is always hope for reform through elective processes. This hope alone is an incentive to prophetic utterance. But in a monarchy reform may mean revolution. The stakes are higher, and the personal losses often greater. Retaliation is generally easier and swifter on the part of monarchical authorities. The possibility of immense personal loss and an ultimate revolution causes many people to become patient rather than prophetic. Conditioned to extol peace over prophecy, many Catholics seal off the spirit of prophecy before it takes roots in their personalities.

It seems that in general a person does not become a prophet overnight. If a person is given to extreme forms of prophetic utterance, it is more than likely that previously he was given to more moderate forms of prophetic utterance, which a democracy would allow. There needs to be a matrix of freedom in which the prophet can develop. Hence, in the United States, because of the freedom that prevails in the secular order, prophets like Groppi and DuBay can develop. In the time of Joan of Arc, the prophet could be more easily stifled; but today Church authorities cannot resort to police power, especially in the United States.

Prophets can arise in a monarchy, but they can last longer in a democracy. It is a mark of discredit to the Church that, when the world is in dire need of prophets to denounce such things as world poverty and the napalming of children, the secular order is a better matrix for the development of prophets than the Church. Of course, it is true that democracy provides no assurance that the radical prophet will be accepted. The people as a whole can be as vicious as their leaders. But if the prophet must be stoned, it seems more fitting that this be done by an unthinking mob than by the leaders of the Church.

It would be a mark of credit to the Church, and in keeping with its prophetic character and the spirit of the Second Vatican Council, if it dropped monarchy and embraced democracy. For then the Church would better manifest its true nature as a community in which the leaders (like Jesus, the Lamb of God) are as gentle as lambs and the people (like Jesus, the Lion of Judah) are as fearless as lions. The Church would then be seen as a community in which the hierarchical lamb can lie down at peace with the prophetic lion.

CONCLUSION

The chief obstacles that might stand in the way of a democratic Church are not in themselves insurmountable. In each case there is a principle inherent in Catholic theology by which the obstacle can be overcome. These principles provide, in effect, emerging rationales for the democratization of the Roman Catholic Church.

The obstacle presented by an idealistic perspective, in which the Church is viewed as perfect and unchangeable, is offset by the existential principle, which implies that the real Church is not only holy, but also sinful and changeable. And because it is sinful and changeable, it ought to be democratic, as democracy seems to be the form of government best able to promote the common good among sinful men and to provide for change.

The obstacle presented by the notion that democracy has never been officially presented as compatible with the Church's teaching is offset by the principle of doctrinal development, which implies that a thing need not be explicit in traditional teaching for it to emerge ultimately into the visible functions of the Church. And because the doctrine of the Church develops as new needs arise, the Church ought to adopt a form of government that allows needs to be quickly perceived. In other words, the Church should adopt a democratic form of government.

The obstacle presented by the argument that revelation and democracy are incompatible is offset by the principle of the equality of the People of God. This principle implies that it is the People of God as a whole that is infallible, not just the magisterium. By assent to the total deposit of revelation, each member of the Church participates in the infallibility of the entire Church. Hence, the decisions of the People of God as a whole are no more liable to impair the faith of the Church than are the decisions of the hierarchy alone. And because the People of God all share a basic equality in the life of faith, a democratic Church is in order. For if all share in the decision making processes, the equality which all share in principle is more likely to be shared in practice.

The obstacle arising from the argument that the hierarchy would not grant the freedom necessary to work for the democratization of the Church is offset by the principle of the personal right to religious freedom. This principle implies that freedom is not bestowed, but that it is a personal and inalienable right. Religious freedom cannot be granted; it can only be exercised. And because the People of God are by nature and grace free people, the Church ought to be a democracy, for a democracy allows a greater exercise of freedom.

The obstacle that would arise if the hierarchy taught (incorrectly) that monarchy is the form of government best suited to meet the contemporary needs of the Church would be offset by the principle of the experiential basis for assent. This principle implies that a teaching set forth by the hierarchy *cannot* be believed if it contradicts the experience of the believer. And because assent is grounded in experience, the Church ought to be a democracy. The Church's purpose is to proclaim the Gospel to the world. But the world is not apt to assent to the Gospel if it is presented in a system of thought or in a language alien to the world. The dialogical process inherent in democracy allows a quicker adaptation of the form in which the Gospel is expressed, making assent more likely.

The obstacle that would arise if the hierarchy established laws against activity leading to a democratic Church would be offset by the principle of the supremacy of conscience. If there are compelling reasons, hierarchical commands need not, and in some cases ought not, be obeyed. And because conscience is supreme in particular situations, the Church ought to adopt a democratic form of government, so that the People of God, sharing in decisions that affect the life of the Church, would be better trained to make decisions for themselves in particular situations where laws and general principles are not in themselves adequate.

The obstacle arising from the argument that democracy will weaken the power of the Church to accomplish its purpose is offset by the principle of subsidiarity, which implies that a more widespread distribution of power will, in effect, provide a larger total aggregate of power with which to achieve the Church's purposes. And because subsidiarity is more likely to be achieved when all the people have a voice in determining structures, a democratic form of government is desirable.

The obstacle arising from the misuse of bureaucratic power to stifle initiative leading toward democracy is offset by the prophetic principle. This principle implies that the word of God uttered by the prophet can expose and frustrate bureaucratic power plays. And because the Church is a prophetic community by nature, it ought to be democratic. For a democracy is more capable than monarchy of providing a matrix of freedom conducive to the maturation of prophets.

In short, the obstacles that might stand in the way of a democratic Church are not irremovable. Further, there are principles inherent in Catholic teaching that provide a theological foundation for the democratization of the Church. In addition, there are compelling reasons why a democracy ought to be established, if the Church is to achieve its purposes. Hence, a Catholic has reason to hope that democracy will become a reality in the Church, and the responsibility to see that it does.

It seems, therefore, that if the faithful are true to their calling, the Church will ultimately adopt a democratic form of government. How soon this happens will depend on two things: the degree to which authoritarianism is entrenched in the hierarchy and the degree to which freedom is exercised by the faithful.

On the one hand, it could be that authoritarianism is so deeply rooted in the Church that a bold display of freedom would trigger a rash of irrational and destructive reactions on the part of the hierarchy. If the hierarchy, jealous of their authority, could be largely unaware of their prophetic responsibilities in the twentieth century, which saw the rise of dictators and the massacre of six million Jews, they could also be largely unaware of their responsibility to cooperate with the exercise of freedom. This could mean, in effect, a conflict more devastating than any of the schisms that divided the Church during the past twenty centuries.

On the other hand, it could be that the desire for freedom is so weak on the part of the vast majority of the People of God that the bold display of freedom by the courageous few might produce a massive conformity to the externals of the Church, particularly the externals of the liturgy. The liturgy, even a well-participated liturgy, could become, instead of a goad to action and a symbol of community, a tranquilizer of prophetic impulses and a vehicle of escape from social responsibilities. Each further display of freedom by the courageous few might produce a greater degree of paranoia on the part of the majority and lead to a widespread rigidity unresponsive to the movement of the Spirit. In such a case the faithful remnant might develop even more rapidly and leave the vast majority behind, stagnating in the structural and liturgical forms of the past and separated from the faithful Church, which would be a tiny minority.

And yet it may be that authoritarianism is no longer a cancer requiring major surgery, but merely a scab on a body that is quickly healing. The Second Vatican Council gives evidence of a healthy body. And it may also be that the desire for freedom, so much in evidence in the body of mankind, will become as vigorous in the Church as it is in much of the world. The articulation of the plight of the poor through modern communications media, the spirit of the civil rights movement, and the drive of the peoples in the developing nations—all these point to a dynamic freedom that could prevail against some of the most powerful technological, social, and political forms of slavery ever to arise in the history of man. And because the Church in general seems to be moving away from monologue into dialogue with the world, it may well enter more fully into a partnership with a developing world community of free men and become a prophet of freedom rather than a party to enslavement.

At any rate, a democratic Church seems to be on the horizon. In adopting democracy, the Church may lose many of its members who have a psychological need for authoritarianism. If the number of such persons would be large, the Church could become a tiny, but faithful, remnant of what was once a gigantic organization. But if the number of such persons would be small, and the rest capable of embracing a greater freedom and a more demanding faith, the Church could become a powerful force (in numbers and in effect) in helping the community of man experience a degree of freedom and fulfillment heretofore unknown. More than likely, however, the Church will find itself somewhere between these two extremes. Whatever its size, the Church will be better off as a democracy, for then its freedom will be more fully realized.

BIBLIOGRAPHY

BOOKS

Abbott, Walter M., S.J. *The Documents of Vatican II.* New York: Guild Press, 1966.

Adam, Karl. *The Spirit of Catholicism.* Translated by Dom Justin McCann, O.S.B. 2d ed. revised. New York: Doubleday & Company, 1954.

Aubert, Roger (ed.). *Historical Problems of Church Renewal.* Vol. VII of *Concilium.* Edited by Edward H. Schillebeeckx, O.P., *et al.* 22 vols. New York: Paulist Press, 1965.

Baum, Gregory, O.S.A. *The Credibility of the Church Today: A Reply to Charles Davis.* New York: Herder and Herder, 1968.

Bedoyere, Michael de la (ed.). *The Future of Catholic Christianity.* Latchworth, Hertfordshire: The Garden City Press, 1966.

————. *The Layman in the Church.* Chicago: Henry Regnery Company, 1955.

Benoit, Pierre, O.P., and Roland E. Murphy, O. Carm. (eds.). *The Human Reality of Sacred Scripture.* Vol. X of *Concilium.* Edited by Edward H. Schillebeeckx, O.P., *et al.* 22 vols. New York: Paulist Press, 1965.

Biechler, James E. (ed.). *Law for Liberty.* Baltimore: Helicon Press, Inc., 1967.

Blau, Peter M. *Bureaucracy in Modern Society.* New York: Random House, 1965.

Blochlinger, Alex. *The Modern Parish Community.* New York: P. J. Kenedy & Sons, 1965.

Bockle, Franz (ed.). *War, Poverty, Freedom: the Christian Response.* Vol. XV of *Concilium.* Edited by Edward E. Schillebeeckx, O.P., *et al.* 22 vols. New York: Paulist Press, 1966.

Buber, Martin. *The Knowledge of Man.* Edited with an introduction by Maurice Friedman. Translated by Maurice Friedman and Ronald Gregor Smith. New York: Harper & Row, Publishers, 1965.

Callahan, Daniel (ed.). *Generation of the Third Eye.* New York: Sheed and Ward, 1965.

————. *Honesty in the Church*. New York: Charles Scribner's Sons, 1965.

————. *The Mind of the Catholic Layman*. New York: Charles Scribner's Sons, 1963.

Caporale, Rock, S.J. *Vatican II: Last of the Councils*. Baltimore: Helicon, 1964.

Catholic Encyclopedia. 15 vols. New York: The Encyclopedia Press, Inc., 1913.

Congar, Yves, O.P. *Lay People in the Church*. Translated by Donald Attwater. 2d ed. revised. Westminster, Maryland: The Newman Press, 1965.

Coriden, James A. (ed.). *We, The People of God*. Huntington, Ind.: Our Sunday Visitor Press, 1968.

Culhane, Eugene K., S.J. *American Catholic Horizons*. New York: Doubleday & Company, 1966.

Dimock, Marshall E. *A Philosophy of Administration Toward Creative Growth*. New York: Harper & Brothers, Publishers, 1958.

Dophner, Julius. *The Questioning Church*. Westminster, Maryland: The Newman Press, 1964.

DuBay, William. *The Human Church*. New York: Doubleday & Company, Inc., 1966.

Duquoc, Christian, O.P. (ed.). *Spirituality in Church and World*. Vol. IX of *Concilium*. Edited by Edward H. Schillebeeckx, O.P., et al. 22 vols. New York: Paulist Press, 1965.

Dyer, Frederick C. and John M. *Bureaucracy Vs. Creativity*. Coral Gables, Florida: University of Miami Press, 1965.

Edelby, Neophytos and Teodoro Jiminez-Urresti (eds.). *Religious Freedom*. Vol. XVIII of *Concilium*. Edited by Edward H. Schillebeeckx, O.P., et al. 22 vols. New York: Paulist Press, 1966.

Geusau, Leo Alting von (ed.). *Ecumenism and the Roman Catholic Church*. Translated by H. J. J. Vaughan, J. S. Harding, and the Documentation Centre. Westminster, Maryland: The Newman Press, 1966.

Gremillion, Joseph. *The Other Dialogue*. New York: Doubleday & Company, Inc., 1965.

Guilday, Peter. *The Life and Times of John England*. 2 vols. New York: The America Press, 1927.

Guitton, Jean. *The Church and the Laity*. Staten Island, N. Y.: Alba House, 1965.

Haring, Bernard, C.Ss.R. *The Law of Christ*. Vol. I: *General Moral Theology*. Translated by Edwin G. Kaiser. Westminster, Maryland: Newman Press, 1961.

————. *The Liberty of the Children of God*. Translated by Patrick O'Shaughnessy, O.S.B. Staten Island, N.Y.: Alba House, 1966.

Harrison, Paul M. *Authority and Power in the Free Church Tradition*. New Jersey: Princeton University Press, 1958.

Houtart, Francois. *The Challenge to Change*. Edited by Mary Anne Chouteau. New York: Sheed and Ward, 1964.

Jiminez-Urresti, Teodoro and Neophytos Edelby (eds.). *Pastoral Reform in Church Government*. Vol. VIII of *Concilium*. Edited by Edward H. Schillebeeckx, O.P., *et al.* 22 vols. New York: Paulist Press, 1965.

Küng, Hans (ed.). *The Church and Ecumenism*. Vol. IV of *Concilium*. Edited by Edward H. Schillebeeckx, O.P., *et al.* 22 vols. New York: Paulist Press, 1965.

————. *The Council in Action*. Translated by Cecily Hastings. New York: Sheed and Ward, 1963.

————. *The Council, Reform and Reunion*. Translated by Cecily Hastings. New York: Doubleday & Company, Inc., 1965.

————. Yves Congar, O.P., and Daniel O'Hanlon, S.J. *Council Speeches of Vatican II*. Glen Rock, New Jersey: Paulist Press, 1964.

———— (ed.). *Do We Know the Others?* Vol. XIV of *Concilium*. Edited by Edward H. Schillebeeckx, O.P., *et al.* 22 vols. New York: Paulist Press, 1966.

————. *Freedom Today*. Translated by Cecily Hastings. New York: Sheed and Ward, 1966.

————. *Structures of the Church*. Translated by Salvatore Attanasio. New York: Thomas Nelson & Sons, 1964.

Lonergan, Bernard, S.J. *Insight: A Study of Human Understanding*. New York: Philosophical Library, 1956.

McKenzie, John L., S.J. *Authority in the Church*. New York: Sheed and Ward, 1966.

Mead, Sidney E. *The Lively Experiment*. New York: Harper & Row, Publishers, 1963.

Merton, Robert K. *et al.* (eds.). *Reader in Bureaucracy*. Glencoe, Illinois: The Free Press, 1952.

Messmer, Sebastian G. *The Works of the Right Reverend John England*. 7 vols. Cleveland, Ohio: The Arthur H. Clark Company, 1908.

Metz, Johannes B. (ed.). *The Church and the World*. Vol. VI of *Concilium*. Edited by Edward H. Schillebeeckx, O.P., *et al.* 22 vols. New York: Paulist Press, 1965.

Montefiore, C. G. and H. Lowe. *A Rabbinic Anthology*. London: Macmillan and Co., Ltd., 1938.

Muller, Alois. *Obedience in the Church*. Translated by Hilda Graef. Westminster, Maryland: The Newman Press, 1966.

Mundy, John and Kennerly McMoody (eds.). *The Council of Constance*. Translated by Louise Ropes Loomis. New York: Columbia University Press, 1961.

Murray, John Courtney, S.J. (ed.). *Freedom and Man*. New York: P. J. Kenedy & Sons, 1965.

————. *The Problem of Religious Freedom*. Westminster, Maryland: The Newman Press, 1965.

———— (ed.). *Religious Liberty: An End and a Beginning*. New York: The Macmillan Company, 1966.

140

THE DEMOCRATIC CHURCH

————. *We Hold These Truths*. New York: Doubleday & Company, Inc., 1964.

Neill, Stephen Charles and Hans-Buedi Weber (eds.). *The Layman in Christian History*. Philadelphia: The Westminster Press, 1963.

New Catholic Encyclopedia. 15 vols. New York: McGraw-Hill Book Company, 1967.

Newman, John Henry. *Certain Difficulties Felt by Anglicans in Catholic Teaching*. 2 vols. London: Longmans, Green, and Co., 1900.

————. *An Essay on the Development of Christian Doctrine*. Introduction by Gustave Weigel, S.J. New York: Doubleday, 1960.

————. *Fifteen Sermons Preached before the University of Oxford*. London: Longmans, Green, and Co., 1898.

————. *An Essay in Aid of a Grammar of Assent*. Introduction by Etienne Gilson. Garden City, New York: Doubleday & Company, Inc., 1955.

————. *The Idea of a University*. Introduction by George N. Shuster. Garden City, New York: Doubleday & Company, Inc., 1959.

————. *A Letter Addressed to His Grace the Duke of Norfolk*. London: B. M. Pickering, 1875.

————. *Parochial and Plain Sermons*. 8 vols. London: Longmans, Green, and Co., 1906.

Nichols, James Hastings. *Democracy and the Churches*. Philadelphia: The Westminster Press, 1951.

Neibuhr, Reinhold. *The Children of Light and the Children of Darkness*. New York: Charles Scribner's Sons, 1960.

Novak, Michael. *The Open Church*. New York: The Macmillan Company, 1962.

Nyiszli, Miklos. *Auschwitz*. Translated by Tibere Kremer and Richard Seaver. Greenwich, Conn.: Fawcett Publications, Inc., 1960.

O'Donoghue, Joseph. *Elections in the Church*. Baltimore: Helicon, 1967.

Rahner, Karl, S.J. *Christian in the Market Place*. Translated by Cecily Hastings. New York: Sheed and Ward, 1966.

————. *Free Speech in the Church*. New York: Sheed and Ward, 1959.

————. *Nature and Grace*. Translated by Dinah Wharton. New York: Sheed and Ward, 1964.

———— (ed.). *The Pastoral Mission of the Church*. Vol. III of *Concilium*. Edited by Edward H. Schillebeeckx, O.P. *et al*. 22 vols. Glen Rock, New Jersey: Paulist Press, 1965.

———— and Herbert Vorgrimler, S.J. *Theological Dictionary*. Translated by Richard Strachan. New York: Herder and Herder, 1965.

————. *Theological Investigations*. Translated with an introduction by Cornelius Ernst, O.P. 2 vols. Baltimore: Helicon Press, 1961.

Riga, Peter. *The Church Renewed*. New York: Sheed and Ward, 1966.

Schillebeeckx, Edward H., O.P. (ed.). *The Church and Mankind*.

Vol. I of *Concilium*. Edited by Edward H. Schillebeeckx, O.P., *et al*. 22 vols. New York: Paulist Press, 1965.

————. *The Layman in the Church*. Staten Island, New York: Alba House, 1963.

———— (ed.). *Man as Man and Believer*. Vol. XXI of *Concilium*. Edited by Edward H. Schillebeeckx, O.P., *et al*. 22 vols. New York: Paulist Press, 1967.

Seven Great Encyclicals. Glen Rock, N. J.: Paulist Press, 1963.

Smith, H. Shelton, Robert T. Handy, and Lefferts A. Loetscher. *American Christianity*. 2 vols. New York: Charles Scribner's Sons, 1963.

Stransky, Thomas F., C.S.P. *Declaration on Religious Freedom of Vatican Council II*. New York: Paulist Press, 1966.

Thorman, Donald. *The Role of the Catholic Layman in America*. New York: Doubleday & Company, Inc., 1965.

Vorgrimler, Herbert, S.J., *Karl Rahner: His Life, Thought and Works*. Translated by Edward Quinn. Glen Rock, N. J.: Paulist Press, 1966.

Weber, Max. *From Max Weber: Essays in Sociology*. Edited and translated by H. H. Gerth and C. Wright Mills. New York: Oxford University Press, 1958.

Wise, John. *A Vindication of the Government of the New-England Churches (1717)*. Introduction by Perry Miller. Gainesville, Florida: Scholars' Facsimiles & Reprints, 1958.

Wolf, Donald J., S.J., and James V. Schall, S.J. (eds.). *Current Trends in Theology*. New York: Doubleday & Company, Inc., 1966.

ARTICLES AND PERIODICALS

Arguett, Robert J. "Is the Parish Council Worthwhile?," *Homiletic and Pastoral Review*, LXVII (May, 1967), 645–649.

Baum, Gregory, O.S.A. "Away from Centralization," *Clergy Review*, XLVIII (May, 1963), 275–279.

————. "The Ecclesial Reality of the Churches," in *The Church and Ecumenism*, edited by Hans Küng, Vol. IV of *Concilium*, edited by Edward H. Schillebeeckx, O.P., *et al*. (22 vols.; New York: Paulist Press, 1965).

————. "Teaching Authority of Vatican II," *Ecumenist*, III (September-October, 1965), 89–93.

————. "Restlessness in the Church," *Ecumenist*, V (March-April, 1967), 33–36.

————. "The Christian Adventure: Risk and Renewal," *Furrow*, XVI (June, 1965), 336–352.

Bertrams, William, S.J. "Subsidiarity in the Church," *Theology Digest*, IX (Spring, 1961), 111–114.

Blehl, Vincent F., S.J. "The Council: A Lesson from the Past," *America*, CVIII (October 27, 1962), 950–952.

Blenkinsopp, Joseph. "On Clericalism," *Cross Currents,* XVII (Winter, 1967), 15–23.

Callahan, Daniel. "The New Freedom," *Commonweal,* LXXXII (June 18, 1965), 401–405.

————. "Preparing for Diversity," *Commonweal,* LXXXII (September 24, 1965), 694–696.

Catholic Messenger. 1966.

Catholic Universe Bulletin. 1967.

Chardin, Teilhard de, S.J. "The Psychological Conditions of Human Unification," *Cross Currents,* III (Fall, 1952), 1–5.

Dalrymple, John. "Obedience and Criticism," *Clergy Review,* LI (September, 1966), 665–678.

Davis, H. Francis. "Newman the Prophet," *Ave Maria,* LXXXIX (March 28, 1959), 22–24.

"Development of Doctrine," *Catholic Mind,* LXV (November, 1963), 3–4.

Fanning, William H. W. "The Church," in *Catholic Encyclopedia* (New York: The Encyclopedia Press, Inc., 1963), Vol. III.

Grealy, John, S.J. "The People of God," *Bellarmine Commentary,* IV (Autumn, 1965), 17–23.

Grisez, Germain G. Review of *Insight: A Study of Human Understanding,* by Bernard Lonergan, S.J., *Thomist,* XXI (October, 1958), 554–560.

Hammans, Herbert. "Recent Catholic Views on the Development of Dogma," in *Man as Man and Believer,* edited by Edward H. Schillebeeckx, O.P., Vol. XXI of *Concilium,* edited by Edward H. Schillebeeckx, O.P., *et al.* (22 vols.; New York: Paulist Press, 1967).

Haring, Bernard, C.Ss.R. "The Law Must Free," *Ave Maria,* XCVIII (September 7, 1963), 16–17.

Hill, Edmund, O.P. "Authority in the Church," *Clergy Review,* L (August, 1965), 619–628.

————. "Authority in the Church II: Development of Institutions," *Clergy Review,* L (September, 1965), 674–685.

"How U.S. Catholics View Their Church," *Newsweek,* March 20, 1967.

Hoyt, Robert. "Dubiously Doubtless," *National Catholic Reporter,* November 9, 1966.

Huising, Peter. "The Reform of Canon Law," in *Religious Freedom,* edited by Neophytos Edelby and Teodoro Jiminez-Urresti, Vol. XVIII of *Concilium,* edited by Edward H. Schillebeeckx, O.P., *et al.* (22 vols.; New York: Paulist Press, 1965).

John XXIII. "Meditations for the Council," *The Pope Speaks,* VIII (Autumn, 1962), 131–137.

Kauffman, Christopher. "The Style of Revolution," *Continuum,* V (Winter-Spring, 1967), 184–186.

Küng, Hans. "And after the Council?," *Commonweal,* LXXXII (September 3, 1965), 619–623.

Leger, Paul Emile. "The Church and Mankind," *Jubilee,* XIII (September, 1965), 16–20.

Lonergan, Bernard, S.J. "The Transition from a Classicist World-View to Historical Mindedness," *Law for Liberty*, edited by James E. Biechler (Baltimore: Helicon Press, Inc., 1967).

Lynch, William F. "The Problem of Freedom," *Cross Currents*, X (Spring, 1960), 97–114.

Martin, Bernard. "Force and Persuasion: Alfred North Whitehead's Philosophy of History," *Ohio University Review*, VIII (1966), 22–43.

Meany, John. "The Use of Authority," *America*, CXIV (March 26, 1966), 409–411.

McKenzie, John L., S.J. "Authority and Power in the New Testament," *Catholic Biblical Quarterly*, XXVI (October, 1966), 413–422.

Muller, Alois. "Authority and Obedience in the Church," in *War, Poverty, Freedom: the Christian Response*, edited by Franz Bockle, Vol. XV of *Concilium*, edited by Edward H. Schillebeeckx, O.P., et al. (22 vols.; New York: Paulist Press, 1966).

Murchland, Bernard G., C.S.C. "The Prophetic Principle," *Commonweal*, LXXXIV (April 29, 1966), 171–175.

Murray, John Courtney, S.J. "The Declaration on Religious Freedom: Its Deeper Significance," *America*, CXIV (April 14, 1966), 592–593.

———. "Religious Liberty and Development of Doctrine," *Catholic World*, CCIV (February, 1967), 277–283.

National Catholic Reporter. 1967.

"Newman as a Modern Father of the Church," *Tablet*, CCXVIII (July 18, 1964), 814.

Newman, John Henry. "On Consulting the Faithful in Matters of Doctrine," *Cross Currents*, II (Summer, 1962), 69–97.

Nicholl, Donald. "The Layman and Ecclesiastical Authority," *Clergy Review*, XLIX (July, 1964), 393–415.

Nogar, Raymond J., O.P. "The Emergence of the Person in Natural Law Theory," *Chicago Studies*, V (Spring, 1966), 81–92.

O'Donoghue, Joseph. "Elections in the Church," *Commonweal*, LXXXII (May 21, 1965), 281–284.

O'Hanlon, Daniel, S.J. "What Can Catholics Learn from the Free Churches?," in *Do We Know the Others?*, edited by Hans Küng, Vol. XIV of *Concilium*, edited by Edward H. Schillebeeckx, O.P., et al. (22 vols.; New York: Paulist Press, 1966).

———. "The Nature, Extent and Style of Authority in the Church," *Law for Liberty*, edited by James E. Biechler (Baltimore: Helicon Press, Inc., 1967).

O'Rourke, James, C.C. "Newman's 'Illative Sense,'" *Irish Ecclesiastical Review*, LXI (March, 1963), 193–199.

Orsy, Ladislas. "Government in Religious Life," supplement to *The Way*, II (May, 1966), 90–107.

Palms, Charles, C.S.P. Review of *On Consulting the Faithful in Matters of Doctrine*, by John Henry Newman, edited by John Coulson, *Catholic World*, CIC (February, 1963), 317–318.

Paul VI. " 'Rerum Novarum' Today," *The Pope Speaks*, XI (Summer, 1966), 324–329.

———. "The Lay Apostolate," *The Pope Speaks*, IV (Summer, 1957), 119–134.

"The Pope's Authority," *Tablet*, CCXX (June 11, 1966), 663–664.

Rahner, Karl, S.J. "The Church of Sinners," *Cross Currents*, I (Spring, 1951), 64–67.

Reilly, Joseph J. "The Present Significance of Newman," *Thought*, XX (Spring, 1945), 389–395.

Richard, Robert L., S.J. "Rahner's Theory of Doctrinal Development," *Catholic Theological Society Proceedings*, XVIII (1963), 157–189.

Ruether, Rosemary. "Father DuBay and the Priest's Union," *Continuum*, V (Winter-Spring, 1967), 182–184.

Rule, Philip C., S.J. Review of *On Consulting the Faithful in Matters of Doctrine*, by John Henry Newman, edited by John Coulson, *Review for Religious*, XXI (September, 1962), 472.

Scharper, Philip. "Is It Time to Overhaul the Pyramidical Structure of Authority in the Church?," *Critic*, XXIII (October-November, 1964), 38–39.

Schillebeeckx, Edward H., O.P. "The Concept of Truth and Related Problems," in *Ecumenism and the Roman Catholic Church*, edited by Leo Alting von Geusau, translated by H. J. Vaughan, J. S. Harding, and the Documentation Centre (Westminster, Maryland: The Newman Press, 1966).

———. "The Layman in the Church," *Thomist*, XXVII (April, 1963), 262–283.

Sillem, Edward A. "Cardinal Newman's *Grammar of Assent* on Conscience as a Way to God," *Heythrop Journal*, V (October, 1964), 377–401.

Stephenson, Anthony A., S.J. "Cardinal Newman and the Development of Doctrine," *Journal of Ecumenical Studies*, III (Fall, 1966), 463–485.

Sullivan, Oona. Review of *On Consulting the Faithful in Matters of Doctrine*, by John Henry Newman, edited by John Coulson, *Jubilee*, IX (March, 1963), 50–51.

Swidler, Arlene. "The Male Church," *Commonweal*, XXIV (June 24, 1966), 387–389.

Tierney, Brian. "Roots of Constitutionalism in the Church's Own Tradition," *We, The People of God*, edited by James A. Coriden (Huntington, Ind.: Our Sunday Visitor Press, 1968).

Tonner, P. J. "Infallibility," in *Catholic Encyclopedia* (New York: The Encyclopedia Press, Inc., 1913). Vol. VII.

Vawter, Bruce. "Recent Literature on the Prophets," in *The Human Reality of Sacred Scripture*, edited by Pierre Benoit, O.P., and Roland E. Murphy, O. Carm., Vol. X of *Concilium*, edited by Edward H. Schillebeeckx, O.P., *et al.* (22 vols.; New York: Paulist Press, 1965).

Wallace, Cecilia. "Ordained Women: an Imperative," *Continuum,* IV (Spring, 1966), 145–147.

Whitson, Robley Edward. Review of *On Consulting the Faithful in Matters of Doctrine,* by John Henry Newman, edited by John Coulson, *Thought,* XXXVIII (Spring, 1963), 148.

Wills, Gary. "The Most Dangerous Man," *National Review,* XIII (October 23, 1962), 319–320.

Wright, John J. "Reflections on Conscience and Authority," *Critic,* XXII (April-May, 1964), 11–15.

UNPUBLISHED MATERIAL

Johnson, Robert. "The Changing Status of the Negro in American Life." Report to NAIRO consultative conference, January 21, 1960.